The Comprehensive Columbia
LSAT
Guide

**A picture
is worth more
than you
think.**

About the Author

Jonathan Van Ee scored in the top 1% on the LSAT, attended Columbia Law School, and has practiced law in New York City and in Silicon Valley, California. For this book, he interviewed both educators and test takers of some of the most difficult standardized tests, including the California and New York Bar Exams (both of which he has also passed) and the LSAT.

Mr. Van Ee has a diverse background, having grown up in Mexico and worked in Russia, Canada, China and France. He has an art hobby, and his art can be seen at www.jonathanvanee.com. This book is the product of Mr. Van Ee's intensive research, broad experience, and careful analysis of the LSAT.

This book is available in hardcopy and e-book versions through
www.comprehensivecolumbia.com

Comprehensive internet LSAT resources are at:
www.comprehensivecolumbia.com
Information on how to earn a commission on sales for people you refer a book to can be found at that website.

I would like to thank my classmates, Oliver Chee, Seth Wiener and Jasper Nzedu, for their advice and encouragement.

Published by The Jonathan Van Ee Company, LLC
© 2006 by Jonathan Van Ee
ISBN 978-1-4303-0311-4

Table of Contents

I. THIS BOOK IS THE BEST TOOL FOR A HIGHER SCORE

This book is a product of my journey to becoming a really good test taker. I explain not just exam basics, but also what the exam booklet of a great test taker will look like after they have taken the LSAT (It is in Appendix F, if you're curious). I will also show you the process of how you can become the best test taker you can be. That is why this is a comprehensive book.

One lesson I have learned is that your initial results on practice LSAT exams are not a reference point for what you can ultimately achieve. This book will help you discover what your abilities really are.

A. How Important Is Your Score On The Exam?

It can be more important than all the grades throughout all your college years. Law schools may give more weight to your LSAT score than to any other single factor for one reason: it is the only tool they have to compare their diverse applicant pool with the same yardstick. Each college and university (and professors within colleges and universities) have different methods for measuring performance. The LSAT's main purpose is to develop a single yardstick with which to measure that diverse applicant pool – that's why it's called a *standardized* test.

You should prioritize your efforts in light of the importance of your LSAT score. Don't be misled by the fact that it's only one exam and takes only one morning to complete. It is one of the biggest events at the beginning of your legal career.

B. Capturing The Hope Diamond

While the LSAT is an important event in your legal career, it may seem tedious, uninteresting and difficult. It is an abstract mental exercise, the culmination of which involves filling in circles on a mechanically graded answer sheet. Don't think of it that way. This is serious stuff.

Your preparation can be more productive if you think of the exam in terms that are interesting to you. Consider the following analogy that I thought of when I studied for the exam.

One of the most valuable objects, the Hope Diamond, has been hidden and is guarded by a hostile regime. Your task is to capture the diamond, which is kept in a highly guarded repository with a wide variety of advanced security measures. For this task you must exhaustively study the repository's structure, its defenses, and anything in it that you can use for your mission. You train yourself physically and mentally to handle the stress and the need for quick thinking. You know exactly which clothing and tools you'll take with you. In the weeks and months before the mission you exercise, practice, and follow a strict diet that will enable you to be in optimal shape on the day you set out to capture the priceless diamond.

On the day of your mission, you leave your base and follow a carefully charted route to the repository. You get through a series of tall, barbed wire fences guarding its perimeter and break in with a special code. One security measure inside the building is triggered when an object crosses a light beam. You use a spray to identify exactly where the beam is and go around it. Your timing is impeccable to avoid the guards and security cameras.

Even though you've never been inside, you know your way around the respository as well as the house you grew up in. You have studied its every detail. The parts of the building that you don't know with precision, such as the position of a chair or the exact width of a hallway, are not an obstacle because you know how to adapt. Also, if something goes wrong (for example, a guard sees you), you have a contingency plan. You are guided by your instincts.

After navigating a series of corridors and rooms, you reach the large chamber housing the diamond. You pour specially engineered oil on the floor to make it slick. You get on your belly to avoid all the security measures, and slowly slide across the floor. The carefully positioned explosive device you place on the thick steel case housing the diamond detonates, you seize the diamond, and escape.

This story is analogous in many respects to your LSAT mission. The Hope Diamond represents the highest score you are capable of. That score is protected and hidden by the examiners through a series of tricky questions with convoluted facts and distracting answer choices. To get that score, you need to train, study the structure of the exam, and have tools (which you will find in this book) that will help you engage questions designed to trick you. When you take the exam, you will feel as if you have already read it because you have studied it exhaustively. The parts of it that you haven't specifically studied are not an obstacle because you know how to adapt to them. Your sense of timing is refined to deal with strict time constraints. When the mission is over, you will have one of the most important elements of your early legal career: the best score you are capable of achieving.

Let's prepare for the mission.

C. Basic Training
Here is some basic information about the exam.

1. *Exam Mechanics*
The exam has four graded sections and one ungraded section, each of which is roughly 25 questions long. Two of the four graded sections have short logic questions. One graded section is made up of "logic games" with sets of questions about deductions and inferences that can be made from the rules of each game. Finally, the reading comprehension section has groups of questions about facts, inferences and conclusions that can be made from passages in that section. The ungraded section will be in the format of one of the above sections. You will probably not be able to tell which section is ungraded, so you should treat all five sections as if they were graded.

2. *The Exam Tests Thinking Ability*
The LSAT tests your ability to think, not your substantive knowledge of law or any other field of learning. The exam does this by asking you to make deductions or inferences based on certain facts. You must manipulate the information in the manner requested in each question, and select the accredited response from five possible responses.

3. *Don't Give Up!*
Scores on your first practice exams are probably not a true reflection of your test taking ability. So don't give up if you initially do not do well!

There are two factors that go into your score on this exam: your natural ability to take these kinds of exams, and the exam taking skills you learn. In sociology these two factors are referred to as "nature" and "nurture." "Nature" is the natural test taking ability you were born with. "Nurture" is the conditioning you go through both at the dinner table in your formative years and through reading this study guide. The debate among sociologists over exactly what constitutes "natural" ability and which abilities are the product of "nurture," is unsettled.

Don't try to settle that debate yourself! Don't be intimidated by this exam if you do not do well initially! It is possible that you simply have not been exposed to the nurture that will make you a much better test taker. After applying the exam taking techniques found in this book you will have the nurture you need. That nurture, combined with your natural exam taking ability, will enable you to attain the highest score you are capable of reaching.

4. *Success Stories*

Success stories were one of the most powerful sources of encouragement in my exam preparation. Consider these two stories.

a. "Could use some improvement" to put it mildly

I know a person with the following set of facts:

  i.   He was one of two students out of a kindergarten class of about 20 people who could not read by the end of kindergarten.
  ii. While growing up, he lost so many things that his mother would tell him that, if his head were not screwed on, he would lose it also.
  iii. He repeated first grade. The second time he took first grade, the class was organized according to academic ability. So, the "A" students sat in the A row, the "B" students in the B row, and so on. The best student sat at the front of the A row. This person sat at the back of the F row for the first few months of the second time he took first grade.
  iv. He failed an ambulance driver test two times and passed on the third try.
  v.   On a diagnostic LSAT exam he scored a little higher than you would expect to score by guessing. The score was so low that the instructor administering the diagnostic exam said test takers with that score should think of doing something else with their life.

b. A genius

Contrast those facts with the story of this person:

  i.   He easily became a member of Mensa.
  ii. On the first try, he passed an exam that Albert Einstein failed.
  iii. On more than one occasion in third grade, he was ranked number one academically in a class of about 50 students.
  iv. He obtained a 4.0 G.P.A. in each of his three undergraduate majors.
  v.   He could speak English and Spanish fluently and was conversant in French.

Those two stories are of the same person. They are my story. I can explain some of the above points further. But, to this day, how much of my success is the result of natural ability is a mystery to me.

I am most qualified to help you improve your exam performance because I am, by far, the most improved test taker I have ever heard of. I scored in the top 1% of test takers not because I was good at it right from the beginning, but because I learned how to take the exam. In this book, I have charted a course for you to improve your score by using the many lessons I have learned.

I wanted to become an attorney. So, I went to Washington D.C. in search of an internship with a law firm. With my superior undergraduate grades I landed an internship at a law firm with offices overlooking the Potomac river in Georgetown, a tony part of metropolitan Washington, D.C. (By the way, while I received a 4.0 G.P.A. *in each of my three majors*, my *overall* G.P.A. was slightly lower). The firm handled international trade issues, which was something I wanted to do.

I wanted nothing more than to attend a good law school and become an attorney.

My plans were dealt a huge blow when I obtained an unbelievably bad score on a diagnostic LSAT exam.

I was dead set on becoming an attorney. Firmly believing I had the abilities required for the job, I put off taking the exam for one year. I studied on weekends and in pockets of time that I created. During that time, I traveled from the lowest rungs of test taking ability to its upper reaches.

I did not know Spanish when my parents moved to Mexico and placed me in a Mexican first grade class. That is why I repeated first grade. Albert Einstein failed the New York Bar Exam, which has become more difficult since he took it. I passed it on my first try. I was probably more prepared than he was. The ambulance exam had a written section and a driving section. I passed the written section on the first try and failed the driving part twice (and passed that part on the third try). That convinced me to make a living with my abstract thinking abilities and not my driving skills.

Albert Einstein did not let his exam failure keep him from using his intellect. You should not let your past performance record keep you from doing your best on the LSAT.

My mother has been a tremendous inspiration to me. She is also aware of many of my shortcomings, including the fact that while growing up I lost many things. My shortcomings were not indications I couldn't do well on the LSAT. You must also be critical of your shortcomings, but not assume that they all reflect badly on your exam-taking ability.

5. *Consider This*

If you are content doing reasonably well in life, you may consider talking to people who know you. After playing board games and otherwise talking with you, what do they think your potential is? Being unhindered by past negative messages you may have received, these people may better appreciate your strong points. That was certainly the case for me.

Before college I took an unofficial ACT and scored roughly in the top 25% of test takers. A cousin of mine was curious about my test score because she thought it would be really high. Upon learning my score, she immediately indicated that I could do much better. But, I was reasonably happy with my score.

Then, after my first year of college, another cousin (who is a sister to the first cousin) asked me what my G.P.A. was. She was curious because she thought it would be really high. I told her my overall G.P.A. at the time was 3.5. Again, I was reasonably happy with this performance. Like my other cousin, she thought I could do much better. I asked her what she thought an acceptable G.P.A. for me would be. She indicated that the *minimum* grade point average I should get was a 4.0.

Today, I think of that conversation as a "kick in the pants." It propelled me to do much better, even though I didn't actually work much harder in each college course. I paid closer attention and studied with more focus on doing well on tests. From then on, I got all A's, with the exception of one B in my final semester of college.

6. *Consistent Errors On A Consistent Exam*

The best single quality of the exam is that it is consistent. It is designed to be one standard with which to compare test takers who have taken the exam at different times. The exam is so consistent that the examiners sell, for training purposes, copies of the exam that date back *several* years. In a book copyrighted in 2004 and for sale in 2006 the examiners sold a test administered in 1992. That was about 14 years earlier and 50 exams before the exams in 2006! The book is entitled "10 Actual, Official LSAT PrepTests" and is published by the Law School Admissions Council, which administers the LSAT.

Fortunately for the LSAT student, test takers consistently make the same mistakes on the exams. Thus, the examiners are able to generate a consistent bell curve even though they administer an exam that does not change significantly over time. Your goal is to understand the areas of the exam where you make mistakes and not repeat those mistakes. That is how you distinguish yourself from other test takers. While identifying mistakes is not pleasant, it is an essential step toward eliminating them.

Most people do not enjoy focusing on their mistakes. One of the most powerful test preparation techniques is to think of your exam taking shortcomings as opportunities. Your shortcomings are like strangers that irritate you. Once you meet and understand them, they become your friends. You can make a shortcoming become a strength when you understand it and turn it around.

D. Structuring Your Plan Of Attack

How you study for this exam depends on the level of priority you give it, your natural ability to take the exam, and the speed with which you improve with practice.

I have prepared three model study plans that you can adjust to your circumstances. Appendix A contains a crash course for people with little time to spend preparing for the exam. Appendix B contains a standard study plan, and Appendix C has an exhaustive plan. Appendices B and C explain how this book should be used in conjunction with previously administered exams that you can purchase. Appendix C contains an explanation for how you can use this book in conjunction with practice exams created by companies that teach the LSAT.

After you have read this book, you will have a better idea about how to plan your approach for this exam. Take the practice exam in Appendix D. Answers and explanations are in Appendix E. Your goal is to apply test taking skills in a manner that is reflected on the "Model Test Booklet" that is in Appendix F. That booklet shows roughly how the practice exam should look after you take it. If you look through it before you take the exam, try not to remember which answers are correct for each question. To avoid confusion, the Model Test Booklet also does not contain diagramming errors. Examples of how to correct diagramming errors are found in Section IV.B.6.d entitled "Advanced Diagramming".

II. TOOLS FOR ATTACKING THE ENTIRE EXAM

The tools in this section apply to the entire exam. You should know and internalize them. Mastering the exam is like learning a language, and these tools help you understand the LSAT's language. When you take the exam, you should be able to read and respond to the

LSAT's language fluently, fully utilizing these techniques while not necessarily being conscious of them.

In later sections we will build on many of the concepts in this section.

A. Time Is Money, and LSAT Time Is Expensive

Time management is probably the biggest element that distinguishes good test takers from others. This is because almost everyone could answer each of the questions correctly if they were given enough time to do so. Only those who answer correctly *within the time allotted* get the higher scores. Each second on the exam is more significant than other seconds in your professional development because your LSAT score can be more significant than all your college grades and all your work experience. Thus, time management is essential.

Here is how you can use your time as efficiently as possible.

1. *Prioritize*

Taking the exam is like moving a pile of rocks of varying sizes and getting one point for each rock moved, regardless of its size. You first move the small ones and, when you're warmed up, you move the large ones. Thus, first try to get easier questions right and then work on the tougher ones.

Your goal is to tackle an entire set of questions in 35 minutes regardless of how long it takes to answer each question. This is because some questions are more difficult than others. You need to do the easy questions first, both because you are more likely to get them right and because they take less time. Then, you need to tackle the harder questions. The easy and hard questions are mixed in with each other, so one skill you need to develop is the ability to differentiate between easy and difficult questions.

You should develop judgment, through practice, of when you know you have answered a question to the best of your ability. When you reach that point, you can quickly move on to the next question.

Many test takers may not finish questions in time, even if they practice extensively. For those people, the skill of prioritizing which questions they will tackle is especially important. They should focus on answering the easier exam questions and then guess on difficult questions.

Other test takers will be able to finish questions in less than the allotted time. If you find you are in that group, make sure you do in fact perform at that level. Don't take the full 35 minutes just because the examiners give them to you. Do the questions quickly, and then relax your mind.

Some questions are not difficult, but take time because they are lengthy. You should do them right after the easy questions because you will probably get them right. Hard questions will also take you more time, but you won't necessarily get them right. If you run out of time, you want to guess on those hard questions.

Your goal is to maximize your score on the entire exam, which means you should pick up as many points as possible, regardless of which parts of the exam they are on. Law schools are not told which sections you did best on, so it doesn't matter where you pick up your points.

If you feel you cannot improve much on one section, such as the reading comprehension section, don't despair. You don't have to do well on each portion of the exam to get a good overall score. For example, if you get a total of three questions wrong in the logical reasoning and games sections, you can get 8 questions wrong in the reading comprehension section and still score in one of the top percentiles of the exam. You can still be in the score range of elite law schools! Think of this: *you could get 8 questions wrong on a section and still score in a top percentile!* In our example, 8 questions wrong is almost 1/3 of the questions for that section, which is not a whole lot better than guessing – in theory you'd get 1/5 of the questions right by simply guessing. This distribution of right and wrong answers illustrates the importance of focusing your efforts on areas where you think you can best improve.

It is as important to know when you may get a wrong answer on a question as it is to know when you will probably get a right answer. When you run into a question you know you have difficulty with, skip it! Save it for later. When you're finished with questions you know you can get right, return to the questions you've skipped. Try to eliminate some wrong answer choices and then do your best in selecting your response. If you run low on time, then make outright guesses on these questions.

2. *Functional Penmanship*

You must forget a number of things your grade school teacher told you about aesthetically pleasing penmanship. The faster and simpler you can write, the better. All that matters is that you are able to understand what you write as you go through the exam. When you read a question, its facts will be fresh in your mind. In general, do not reproduce in writing things that you know and can keep track of on your own. For example, there will be a rule discussed later in this book that goes like this: "Each event may be scheduled only once." Out of caution, I advise you to write this rule in shorthand. But, if you can answer questions without writing this rule, and without making careless mistakes, then you should not write out this rule.

However, if you do write out this rule, here is one way to do it:

I recruited my mother to write the above example. This is an example of how you should not write this rule. It is way too neat and will take up too much time. Here is how I would write that rule under exam conditions:

I may not be able to understand that writing if I ran across it in a random setting. The "once" could pass for the letters "ovee". Also, I might think the line through "ea" meant something. But, in the context of the exam, I know exactly what the above text means. It will serve as a "tickler" that will remind me exactly what the essential elements of the rule are. I will know that the line through "ea" was a mistake because I was writing the circle too fast.

The handwriting throughout this book is not as sloppy as it could be to fully reflect a skilled test taker's notes. Most people would not understand it if it were that sloppy. The handwritten examples do not reflect neat penmanship either. The quality of the penmanship here is intended to serve as a reminder that you should develop the skill of writing quickly and in a manner that makes sense to you (also, I didn't inherit my mother's good handwriting).

3. *Internalize Test Taking Techniques*

The exam should become so natural that you are not conscious of all the exam taking techniques when you take it. You should know and employ them automatically without necessarily being conscious of the fact that you're doing so.

4. *Transfer Answer Choices In Groups*

Do not transfer questions from the booklet to the answer sheet one at a time. Instead, transfer them in sections. This both saves time and gives your mind a mental break. A good rule of thumb is to transfer all responses for questions that appear on each set of two pages that face each other, regardless of how many questions there are.

5. *Be Conscious Of How You Spend Your Time*

Be conscious of how you spend your time to determine whether all of what you are doing is necessary. If you are able to take shortcuts without compromising your practice test scores, take them.

6. *Discover Your "Cruising" Speed*

After you have mastered the exam-taking techniques in this book and reduce the number of careless mistakes you make, push yourself. While the exam is designed to impose time pressure on people, not everyone feels time pressure on the exam. If you are able to finish the exam in less than the allotted time, do so and then let your mind rest in the extra minutes.

Push yourself until you find you are starting to make careless mistakes. Then, slow down a little so you don't make careless mistakes. This is your "cruising" speed. You need to take the exam as fast as you can, at a sustainable rate, while not making careless mistakes. For tips on how to identify, and deal with, careless mistakes, see "Careless Errors" in section II.D.2.

If you have an issue with making careless mistakes, deal with that issue before you try to improve your speed. If you try to take the exam faster while making the same careless errors, you will simply be spinning your wheels by making unnecessary careless mistakes, only making them faster.

B. The Entire Exam Is Mental

Your state of mind is the most critical element when you take the exam. A positive attitude, which you must keep throughout the exam, will help you to think most clearly.

Your mind is like a muscle. All the practice you do before the exam will strengthen it. However, even strong minds get tired, so you must let your mind rest throughout the exam.

The following techniques will help you to use your mental energy most efficiently. In addition, the points outlined in section VII of this book entitled "Physical Preparations" are critical for mental preparedness.

1. *Confidence Is Critical – Never Lose It, Never*
You must have a razor sharp mindset unhindered by anything throughout the entire exam. When you are unsure of an answer, don't understand a question, or are unable to finish a section you thought you should have finished, it is only human to lose confidence. You must *never* let that happen. Why? Because losing your confidence will not help you choose the best of five answer choices. It will *never* help you.

Losing confidence when you make a mistake, or simply don't understand something, is so natural that you need to make sure it doesn't happen to you. Here are pointers on how to keep your confidence.

Accept yourself. Even when you are doing your best, there are some questions that you will probably get wrong, no matter how hard you try. This is a simple, almost universal, fact that applies to even the best test takers. People who score a perfect 180 may get some questions wrong. You should accept this fact, be at peace with it, and not let it bother you in any manner when you are not sure of an answer.

We all make careless mistakes, and you may make mistakes on the day of the exam. This is another fact you need to accept and not let bother you. When you see a mistake, simply correct it and move on. Think of it as an opportunity that you seized.

Most test takers will have a harder time with certain individual questions and with certain sections of the exam. I have a friend that got every single question right on the reading section but did not do as well in the other sections. He still got into a great law school! Your goal is to achieve the highest overall score that you are capable of.

Compartmentalize your thoughts into each question. With the exception of the analytical games and reading sections, the facts you use to answer one question do not carry over to other questions. Carrying over frustrations from one question to the next will not help, and will only hurt you.

Visualize yourself as a warrior who continues the battle after being wounded. The battle is mental. You have the power to heal yourself as quickly as you are wounded. Charge ahead fearlessly. When you encounter a question you know is difficult for you, CONGRATULATE YOURSELF! Being able to identify which questions you may get wrong is *as important* as being able to identify which questions you will probably get right (see section II.F entitled "What if my scores plateau?" for more on this). Spotting a difficult question enables you to respond accordingly. You can either guess or narrow down the answers through a process of elimination to increase your odds!

Do not let unfamiliar facts intimidate you. The facts will probably be equally unfamiliar to most test takers; and even if a test taker has an in-depth knowledge of a passage's topic, it may work against them. For example, if a certain question concerns the living habits of a sea otter you wrote your dissertation on, be sure to keep your dissertation separate from the facts in the passage! Your knowledge may help you read the passage more easily, but it will work against you if you add facts that are not found in the passage.

2. *Focus Is Critical*

You must focus completely on your task, which is simply to select the best of five answer choices. *Everything* you do must further that goal. Thoughts about anything other than the exam question before you, whether it be from a prior question, from the day before or from an annoying noise your neighbor may make during the exam, must be put to one side. This is a lot to ask of your mind while it is tackling a tricky, and at times boring exam for several hours. Here are a number of ways to stay focused:

a. Do not engage the author

Stay focused despite boring, interesting, and controversial parts of the LSAT. You may get a reading passage in one of the last sections of the exam that articulates a political view you agree with. The author may outline reasons supporting that view that you had not thought of. After a few hours of test taking you're a little tired, and bored, and this material is intriguing. You may be tempted to examine how the author's views are in line with your views and come up with other reasons that support your shared political views. You can't let that happen.

Something you disagree with, or find disturbing, could also cause you to lose focus. You may be tempted to debate the author. This thinking will also cause you to lose precious time by losing focus.

b. Know what is significant

Certain parts of the exam are more significant than others. Generally, question stems and answer choices are more significant than other exam parts. You will substantially increase your ability to identify what portions of questions are significant by reading this book. That ability should then be refined with practice.

c. Use your pencil extensively

Interacting with the questions by underlining key words, rating questions and answer choices (more on this later) is one way to keep your mind engaged. But, don't overdo it by writing things that may be distracting or that do not help you answer a question.

d. Give your mind a break, let it wander

Give your mind a break by consciously letting it wander whenever you can. When transferring your scores, you should think about something other than the exam (without sacrificing any accuracy in transferring the scores). During any breaks you may be given, stand up, walk around, and think about pleasant things unrelated to the exam.

e. If you lose focus, pause

Be on the lookout for when you do lose focus. If it happens, don't let it affect your concentration or your confidence. Simply reign in your mind and keep on plugging. If this doesn't work, pause, take your eyes off the exam, look at the ceiling, turn your body to one side of your chair and then to the other and stretch your arms by pushing your elbows behind your back. Then, dive back into the exam.

f. Remind yourself that you can relax completely when it's over

Attack difficult, intense and boring material by reminding yourself that when it's over you can relax completely.

g. Confine your reasoning to the facts given to you on the exam

Everything you need to respond to the questions is on the exam. The exam does not test substantive law or other areas of learning. Thus, whenever you read a question, do not add facts or assumptions that are not given to you in the questions. You may make reasonable deductions, inferences and other conclusions *based on the facts given*, but you may not rely on information outside those facts.

If, at first, you are not able to differentiate between justified conclusions based on facts given and other conclusions, you should focus on developing that skill through practice. This book contains many techniques for making conclusions that are justified. Knowing those techniques will help you understand what the examiners are asking and what information you can use to answer the question.

h. Focus your studies

Staying focused in the process of preparing for the exam is also important. You may have questions, such as "Why do I need to take this exam?" "Is it a useful exam?" "Is it fair?" "Does it predict success in law school or later on in the legal profession?" These are all interesting questions that have no bearing on how to choose one of the five answer choices for each question on the exam. If you find these questions interesting, leave them for later.

C. Be Careful With Extreme Words

You must pay close attention to words that may seem small but make all the difference in selecting answers. Words like "shall," "never," "always," "only" and "except" all must be given their exact meaning.

When found in an answer choice these words often, though not always, signal a wrong answer that can be eliminated. Keep your eye out for them, give them their full meaning, and eliminate them as answer choices with an "X" if you determine they are not the accredited response.

D. Generate A Rigorous Report Card

You must discover how you operate to improve your performance. The more you understand areas of improvement, the more you will be able to improve. The best tool for that self-analysis is a rigorous report card. Start recording your grades soon because you will probably improve most initially, which is an encouraging thing to see on your report card.

It can be helpful to create a graph that helps you visualize your performance. Here's a model grid upon which you could make such a graph:

Number Correct				
28				
27				
26				
25				
24				
23				
22				
21				
20				
19				
18				
17				
16				
15				
14				
13				
12				
11				
10				
9				
8				
7				
6				
5				
4				
3				
2				
1				
Date: August	1	2	3	4

On this chart you should have two lines, one that shows how many answers you got right and another that shows careless errors. Graphs are helpful because you can instantly visualize how you are doing and see the path you've taken to where you are.

Your report card should contain the entries described below.

1. *The Number of Correct Answers*

This is perhaps the most obvious part of the report card because it is the bottom line. You should always understand why your correct answers are correct and why your wrong questions are wrong. You may have gotten lucky on a question, or found a correct answer for the wrong reason. Those kinds of right answers will not help you on the day of the exam. You must understand the reasoning behind each right response to get consistently right answers.

2. *Careless Errors*

It is important to keep track of the number of careless errors because they can be corrected with a unique set of skills. These errors result from not reading closely. They are where you kick yourself and say "I should have gotten that one right." You don't need to study that kind of question. You need to be more careful so that you get it right the next time. You understand the substance, but need to work on execution. To correct careless mistakes, you may need to work on focusing, double checking some answers, and taking care in transferring your answers to the bubble sheet. Improved time management skills can also give you more time to be careful.

Also, it is important to identify careless errors because they can help you determine whether you're able to take various shortcuts on the exam that are described later on. If you can take a shortcut without making a careless mistake, take it!

You want to eliminate careless errors completely. You should focus on eliminating careless errors just like any other kind of error because a wrong answer is wrong, regardless of the reason –whether it's because you simply didn't understand the question or whether you carelessly answered a question you fully understood.

It is important to eliminate careless errors because they are the simplest to eliminate. You don't have to develop more techniques to analyze a reading section, or learn more diagramming skills to attack a war game.

There are a number of things you can do to minimize careless errors. First, know the fastest speed you are able to operate at without making careless errors. That is the speed you should operate at throughout the exam. Second, double check your work. When you have gone through each section once and transferred your scores (but before you tackle the hard questions you passed over once) double check some of your transferred answers to make sure they were transferred correctly.

The time at which you do this check doesn't necessarily have to be right after you go through the entire section once. If you're losing focus and your mind could use a little break, give it that break by taking a few moments to double check the accuracy of the answers you've already transferred to the answer sheet. Double checking answers is tedious, but does not require much mental muscle. Thus, it can be a form of mental relaxation.

If, when double checking your answers, you find that you have made an error, correct the error and move on. Do not let the error affect your confidence level in any manner. The very reason you are double checking your responses is so that you can catch any errors you may have made! Think of correcting errors this way: you just increased your raw score by one point!

If you find a number of careless errors, you may want to slow down and work on increasing your focus.

3. *The Date*

Dating each score allows you to mark your progress. Initially, your scores will probably steadily increase as you become familiar with the kinds of questions on the exam.

E. Journal

With a journal you can look back and get the big picture by seeing patterns that may develop in the difficulties you have. It can also be encouraging to go back and see how far you have developed. In such a journal you can record significant things you learn or areas in need of improvement.

F. What if my scores plateau?

Your scores will probably hit a plateau, at which point you may consider whether you've reached your full potential for taking the LSAT. It is possible to increase your score after you've reached a plateau, so don't get discouraged simply because your scores do not continue to steadily increase. Here's what you should do.

Take a step back and look at the big picture. Examine which kinds of questions you get wrong. Look for patterns of wrong thinking and correct them, even if it seems unnatural. These patterns may not be apparent to you when you take each set of practice questions, but when you look at your wrong answers as a group, you may be able to see that you get a certain kind of question wrong consistently. Don't get discouraged! This is exactly what you are looking for.

Compare your wrong answer choices to correct answer choices and get a feel for how you must answer these kinds of questions. When you take more practice questions, answer them with your new thinking skills until they become natural.

Do you understand why you get a group of questions wrong? Or, do you simply disagree with the examiners' answers and find yourself unable to come up with the right answers on your own? This can happen with questions in the reading comprehension section. If you agree with a point of view articulated in a reading comprehension passage, you may not perceive the tone of that section as being "harsh." You may simply think it's "forceful" and thereby choose the wrong answer. You could point to various parts of the reading passage to support your view and be unable to pick up, on your own, the correct response.

You can reach a point at which, no matter how sensitive or aware of your own biases you become, you still cannot improve your performance. When you reach that point with certain kinds of questions, move on and focus on improving your score with other kinds of questions that you don't fully understand.

If you are simply unable to adapt your thinking to consistently get more correct responses, don't get discouraged! Your task in studying for the exam is to reach your full potential. When you reach the point at which you can no longer increase your performance by developing your understanding of questions, you have achieved your goal. You know what your potential is.

You also will have established an important guidepost for the exam: you will know how to prioritize questions. You should leave hard questions until last so that you can spend more time on them, or simply guess on them if you run out of time. You still may get them correct 20% of the time, and probably more often if you're able to eliminate some wrong answer choices! Remember, you can obtain a high score even if you get 1/3 of the questions wrong on one *entire* section!

Sometimes in the middle of a plateau, your score may spike, and you will get all the answers correct on a section. Examine why that happened. Was the room you were in especially quiet? Did you have a strong cup of coffee just before doing the questions? Did you clear your mind when you took those questions? Refine your test-taking technique accordingly.

Similarly, if your scores dip, examine why. Were the questions harder overall? Did that set of questions contain more of the kinds of questions that you find difficult? Were you not able to focus on that day?

G. Develop Instincts

The most important thing you will gain through practice is better instincts. Here is how your instincts may develop.

1. *Identify what kind of responses to look for*

The examiners have patterns of accredited responses that go along with the patterns of questions. Being able to gravitate towards such responses will help you eliminate wrong responses.

2. *Focus on important facts*

In a reading comprehension section you'll be able to look for key words that are found not just in the questions associated with the passage, but that usually have a bearing on which response is the correct one.

3. *Know which facts are not important or are irrelevant*

You can increase your speed by skipping over unimportant facts. For example, in war games the exact nature of the objects in the games is not important. The *relationship* between the objects is important. Whether a game concerns houses along a street or cars in a multilevel garage is not usually important. The relationship between the houses and cars is important. Are the blue cars always on the first level? Are the two-story houses to the west of the single story houses?

4. *Sense of timing*

Having a sense of timing is important because it will let you maximize the amount of time you spend on hard questions. You need to move quickly through easier questions and then allocate more time to the difficult ones. If you have time pressure, you should know at what point to stop working on hard questions and move on to guessing. Checking your timepiece and calculating how much time you have consumes time and mental energy.

All of these skills build on each other and allow you to spend more mental energy, and spend it more efficiently, attacking the exam and driving up your score.

III. LOGICAL REASONING: THE LARGEST BLOCK OF ENEMY TERRITORY

The logical reasoning sections contain a series of discreet fact patterns with one, and sometimes two, questions based on those facts. The questions have different structures, the most common of which are described and analyzed below.

You want to excel here because it represents half of the graded portion of the exam. It is difficult to do poorly on the logical reasoning section and recover elsewhere. Also, some skills you develop for this section, such as the use of contrapositives (you will know what this word means later) and diagramming techniques, can carry over to the other sections.

A. The Exam's Directions

Here are the exam's directions for this section. Read and understand them now, because they probably won't change. Don't take time to read them during the exam.

> Directions: The questions in this section are based on the reasoning contained in brief statements or passages. For some questions, more than one of the choices could conceivably answer the question. However, you are to choose the <u>best</u> answer; that is, the response that most accurately and completely answers the question. You should not make any assumptions that are by commonsense standards implausible, superfluous, or incompatible with the passage. After you have chosen the best answer, blacken the corresponding space on your answer sheet.

These directions highlight the most difficult part of this section: you must choose the *best* answer, not simply the correct answer. Sometimes, there may be no right answer, in which case the best answer is the one that is *least wrong*.

Another item highlighted by these directions, which is applicable to the entire exam, is that you should not make assumptions based on material that is not spelled out in the exam itself. You should limit your analysis to the facts given in the questions and to reasonable conclusions based on those facts.

One part of these directions that deserves clarification is how you blacken the spaces on the answer sheet. These directions imply that you should blacken each answer choice right after you have answered each question. As is explained earlier in this book, you should transfer your answers in groups to save time and to give your mind a rest while you transfer groups of answers.

B. Categories of Questions Explained

As you study and practice questions in each of the categories below, keep track of which ones are easier for you. When you take the exam, you want to first do the easier questions, and then the more difficult ones.

1. *Assumption*

Assumption questions ask you to identify a fact that is necessary for a conclusion. These questions usually have a set of facts and then a conclusion about those facts. The conclusion will not flow directly from the facts however. It will depend on additional information. That additional information is the assumption you must identify.

These questions are like the following puzzle:

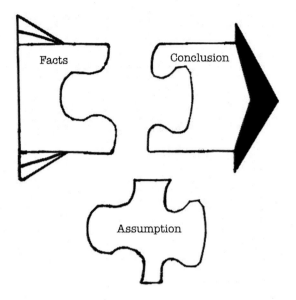

The assumption is the information that best connects the conclusion to the facts. There are valid and invalid assumptions. If the question asks you to identify an assumption, you must do so, even if the author is making an invalid assumption. Here is a practice question:

The Centerville symphony has long played classical pieces composed mostly by Mozart. Critics in the Centerville Press have recently complained that the quality of the symphony's concerts is hindered by a lack of diversity in the composers for the pieces it plays at its concerts. The symphony decided to respond to the critics because last week, it announced its Fall schedule would include concerts containing masterpieces from a wide variety of composers, including J.S. Bach and Handel.

The reasoning above depends on which of the following assumptions:

(A) The varied schedule would not have been adopted were it not for the critics' views.
(B) The critics wanted the symphony to play more pieces by Bach and Handel.
(C) A symphony's performances are of a higher quality when they feature a variety of composers.
(D) The symphony has decided to broaden its scope of music.
(E) The symphony has never before played pieces by J.S. Bach and Handel.

The stem of this question immediately tells you it is an assumption question. The "stem of the question" is this sentence: "The reasoning above depends on which of the following assumptions:"

The facts in this question are found in the first two sentences. The question indicates "The Centerville symphony has long played classical pieces composed mostly by Mozart. Critics in the Centerville press have recently complained that the quality of the symphony's concerts is hindered by a lack of diversity in the composers for the pieces it plays at its concerts."

The conclusion is found in the last sentence, which basically says the symphony has addressed the critics' concern. Your job is to connect the facts to the conclusion with the proper assumption.

The author of this question is drawing a causal connection between what the critics said and what the symphony has done. The author concludes that the critics' views caused the symphony to change the music it plays. For this conclusion to be correct, it must be true that the symphony would not have made such a change if the critics had not expressed their views. Answer choice A is thus correct.

The remaining answer choices are statements that could be true, but they do not directly address the causal connection that the author asserts.

2.   *Parallel-the-Reasoning*

In these questions you must identify an argument's structure and match it with the correct answer choice. The facts in the two arguments will be different, but the argument structure will be similar.

Here is an illustration of a parallel reasoning question:

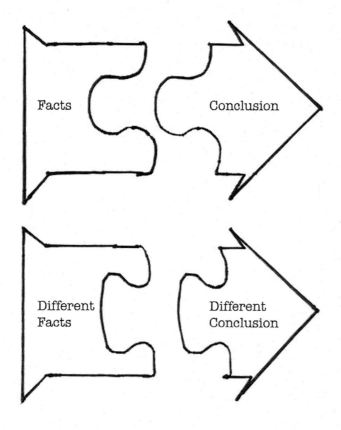

Here is a question:

Big cars are better than small cars because they are safer and have more room. Mr. Peterson has a large old car that is falling apart. He should not buy a new car because new cars are smaller than his old car.

This reasoning is similar to which of the following?

(A) Mice have softer fur if they eat protein and drink plenty of water. Nancy should buy mice food that is rich in protein for her pet mouse.

(B) If land is flat, it is usually suitable for planting. Bill's land is suitable for planting many things, including important crops such as corn and beans. Therefore, his land must be flat.

(C) Big boats take longer to cross Coco Lake and cannot dock everywhere, but they are more efficient. Angie should use a big boat because she wants to cheaply transport a bulky table.

(D) In Victorville snow usually melts in March if there is no snowfall in late February. This year, snow fell in late February, so Sally should not plant her garden until at least April.

(E) Students learn more in classrooms with multimedia presentations that allow them to access more information. Jill should take a biology class offered in a modern classroom instead of one offered by a scholar who uses only a blackboard.

E is the right answer because in E the author takes one aspect of something (multimedia) and bases all decisions on that one aspect. The author does so despite the existence of other reasons for making a different decision. This is similar to the reasoning in the facts given in the question. There, the author uses the size of a car as the only factor to consider, and ignores other factors.

Choice A is incorrect because the author does not suggest that Nancy reject a mouse food. In this question the author rejects small cars. Choice B is wrong because it concerns reasoning about whether something is part of a group, which is different from the reasoning in this question. In choice C the author considers a number of factors to arrive at what could be a prudent decision. This choice is wrong because in the facts of this question the author considers only one factor (the size of cars) to arrive at a questionable decision.

Choice D is wrong because it concerns a conclusion based on an observed pattern.

3. *Conclusion*

Conclusion questions are among the simplest ones. You are given a set of facts and are asked to select a valid conclusion or inference. These questions can be illustrated as follows:

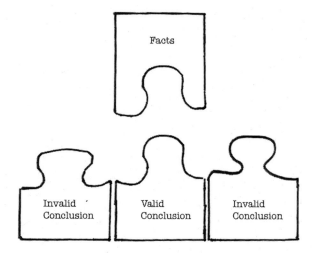

The most important part of these questions is the facts because the conclusion derives from them. You need to check each answer choice against the facts to determine which fits best. Here is a question:

The Ground Palace Theater sells out every weekend on which there are two new releases. Some movies bring in large audiences three weekends after they are released, but most bring in large crowds for one or two weekends. This weekend the theater was not sold out, although it had large audiences.

Which of the following is a valid conclusion about the theater?

(A) There was only one new release this weekend.
(B) The large crowds came to see new releases.
(C) Last weekend the theater was definitely not sold out.
(D) A special promotion attracted the crowds.
(E) A competitor theater went out of business.

Choice A is correct. From the facts one can conclude that large crowds attended the theater on a weekend when there was one new release because it sells out when there are two new releases. The other choices are either wrong or cannot be inferred from these facts. Answer B is wrong because the theater *sells out* when there are releases. Here, the theater did not sell out. Choice C is wrong because there is nothing in the facts to establish conclusively that the theater was not sold out last weekend (although under these facts it is possible that it was not sold out that weekend). Choices D and E are both wrong for the same reason.

4. *Inference*

Inference questions will give you a set of facts from which you must arrive at a conclusion or inference. This figure illustrates how these questions work:

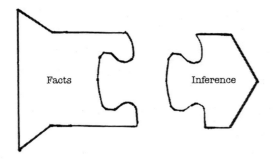

Here is an example:

In five years the Roseville community will use more water than is available from existing water sources. Then, the different sectors of the Roseville community that consume water, which include residential, commercial and industrial users, will have to conserve water. The mayor of Roseville has unveiled a water conservation program. Among other things, in five years it will ration water in proportion to the needs of each sector in the community. In anticipation of the rationing, some residents are expanding their current use of water by installing swimming pools and by irrigating their yard more.

Which of the following must be true about the mayor's approach?

(A) It is fair because it allocates water in proportion to the community's needs.
(B) It will not effectively control water usage.
(C) Commercial and industrial users will get less water than they need.
(D) It can give people an incentive to use more water, rather than conserve it.
(E) It will fail because it will not develop additional sources of water.

This question gives us a set of facts and the answer choices represent inferences. Your job is to find the inference that most closely fits the facts. Answer choice D is correct here, because it most directly flows from the facts. The other answer choices may be true, but they do not follow as closely from the facts as answer choice D.

Answer choice A is wrong because the facts do not tell us the proportion of the needs of the community's sectors. Answer choice B is wrong because there is no indication in the facts that the conservation approach will not effectively limit the use of water. The program is potentially ineffective in that it may not arrive at a proper allocation of water to each sector of the community, but that consideration is most directly addressed in answer choice D. Answer choice C is wrong because there is no indication in the passage of how much water industrial and commercial users will need. One can conclude that, when residential users inflate their needs, this must necessarily mean that other users will get less than what they need. That is a valid conclusion, but it is most directly addressed in answer choice D.

Answer choice E is wrong because the facts do not tell us anything about sources of water, including information about whether they can be developed.

5. *Flaw*

Some questions will ask you to identify the flaw in the author's reasoning. These questions will have facts and an erroneous conclusion about those facts. Here is an illustration of a question about a flawed argument:

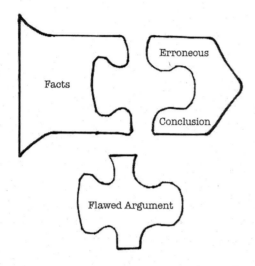

It is important to understand the erroneous conclusion because it will help you identify the flawed reasoning that it is based upon. Here is a question:

> Muscular swimmers can withstand the cold waters and strong undercurrents of the Rough River. Swimming across the river, the most common means for crossing it, is a dangerous rite of passage for the people who live along its banks. Not all who try are able to swim across. Thus, anyone who wants to cross the Rough River must endure an intense exercise regime and maintain a healthy diet.

This reasoning is flawed because:

(A) Swimming is not the only way the river can be crossed.
(B) Some people can become muscular swimmers without maintaining a healthy diet.
(C) The river probably has fords that can be safely crossed by many healthy people.
(D) Some people who intensely exercise and keep a healthy diet will still not be able to swim across the river.
(E) More than exercise and healthy dieting are required to swim across the dangerous river.

Choice A is correct. The author ignores the fact that the river can be crossed in more than one way. This question's statement that swimming is "the most common means" for crossing the river, implies there are other means for crossing. B is wrong because the issue is whether a person can cross the river, not whether they can become muscular swimmers. Choice C is wrong because it is not a warranted inference. It is possible that the Rough River does not have fords that can be safely crossed. Answers D and E are wrong because, while they establish ways the reasoning could be flawed, they are not specifically supported by the facts in the question.

6. *Weaken the argument*

In "weaken the argument" questions you will be asked to identify the response that calls into question a conclusion. The conclusion is the "argument" that is weakened. You need to understand exactly what the argument is because the correct response attacks *the argument*.

These questions can be illustrated as follows:

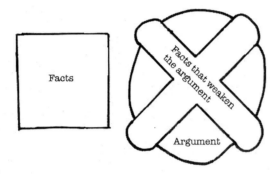

Here is a question:

Snowmobiles are light, fast, and versatile. Snowmobile manufacturers have lowered the noise emitted by the snowmobiles they produce and have increased their fuel efficiency. Therefore, the Peak Point mountain community would benefit from the widespread use of snowmobiles.

The above reasoning would be weakened if:

(A) Extensive use of snowmobiles would seriously damage the fragile mountain ecosystem that Peak Point depends on.
(B) Peak Point does not always have snow.
(C) Despite the advances, snowmobiles remain noisy and inefficient compared to other forms of winter transportation.
(D) Communities in mountain regions do not always need a light, fast and versatile form of transportation.
(E) Snowmobiles are best suited for use in flat, not mountainous, regions.

This question gives us some positive information about snowmobiles, and then concludes "Therefore, the Peak Point mountain community would benefit from the widespread use of snowmobiles." We need to find information that attacks this argument. Choice A most directly attacks the argument because it establishes the opposite conclusion: snowmobiles would not benefit Peak Point.

Choice B does not directly attack the argument. Peak Point could still benefit from snowmobiles even if it does not always have snow. Choice C is not directly on point. The conclusion at issue here concerns whether Peak Point will benefit from snowmobiles, not the merits of snowmobiles relative to other forms of transportation. Choice D is too extreme and too broad. The conclusion is only about Peak Point, not mountain communities in general. The issue is not whether those communities "always need" snowmobiles. Choice E is wrong because, like choice C, it discusses a comparison that is not on point.

7. *Principle*

Principle questions will ask you to apply a principle to facts or reasoning. It is important to understand with precision the principal at issue, so you may want to read it twice. Here is an illustration of the structure of these questions:

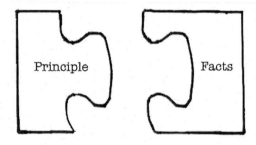

Here is a question:

Many excellent soccer players in Flevoville become reasonably good baseball players because more people attend baseball games. Those soccer players are like a master painter who sacrifices the quality of her art to please the masses. Such people are shortsighted because some great people are only appreciated many years after their death.

1. The above reasoning most closely conforms to this principle:

(A) People can be great, whether or not they are appreciated during their lifetime.
(B) Athletes and artists have a better idea of what quality is than do their audiences.
(C) People should focus their efforts on what they excel at, not on attaining fame during their lifetime.
(D) Popular people are sell-outs who sacrifice quality to gain recognition.
(E) Greatness does not depend on whether your audience appreciates you.

The facts of this question describe a situation in which people who are really good at one thing do something else because it is more popular during their lifetimes. Answer choice C most closely follows this reasoning. It urges the reader to do two critical things that are also found in the facts of the question: 1) do what you are good at; and 2) do so even if you do not attain fame during your lifetime.

Answer choice A is incorrect because it does not specifically deal with the choice of people who in fact are great, to do what they are great at. Answer choice B is incorrect because the question does not deal with who decides what a quality performance is, but rather on whether a performance should be made at all based on its popularity.

Answer choice D is incorrect because the question does not judge popular people. In fact, the question implies that popularity is good because it indicates that it would be a good thing for a person to be popular after their lifetime. Answer choice E is wrong for roughly the same reason. The question's facts imply that recognition or appreciation after a person's lifetime is a good thing.

Here is another question that relates to the same fact pattern:

2. The above reasoning assumes:

(A) Master painters sacrifice the quality of their art to attain public recognition.
(B) Popular recognition is a good thing, regardless of when it occurs.
(C) Recognition of one's abilities after one's death is not as satisfying as being recognized during one's lifetime.
(D) The excellent soccer players would be appreciated at some point in time if they played soccer.
(E) Residents of Flevoville do not appreciate good soccer or quality art.

Here, answer choice D is correct. By calling the players "shortsighted" and by indicating that some people are only appreciated after their death, the author assumes that the players will be appreciated after their death. If they are not appreciated after their death, then they would not have been "shortsighted".

Answer choice A is incorrect because the question does not concern master painters. Answer choice B is not the correct choice, even though it is a true statement. Answer choice D is a better statement because it specifically relates to soccer players.

Answer choice C, while perhaps generally true, is not an assumption made by the facts of the question. In fact, it is inconsistent with the question's implication that recognition after one's death is as satisfying as recognition during one's lifetime. Answer choice E is incorrect because the question concerns what is popular, not what is appreciated in Flevoville. Also, while the question uses an analogy to a "master painter" it says nothing of whether the residents in Flevoville appreciate such people.

8. *Strengthen the Argument*

These questions are the inverse of "Weaken the Argument" questions. Here is a question:

> The Cave Club has long sought to protect the natural treasures found in caves by increasing public awareness of those treasures. Recently, the state approved a plan to build a freeway connecting two large cities. This freeway will cross over a section of a cave with large crystals that have developed over thousands of years. The Cave Club opposes this plan because it would place the crystals in danger of being destroyed.
>
> The Club's argument would be strengthened if:
>
> (A) Roads have been built over many caves with these crystals, and each time the crystals have been destroyed.
> (B) The state did not perform an in-depth study of the routes available for the freeway.
> (C) The endangered crystals are not found anywhere else in the world.
> (D) There is another route available for the freeway that does not cross over the cave.
> (E) Another freeway is not necessary because there already is a freeway connecting the two cities.

Choice A strengthens the Club's argument because it establishes a pattern that could be repeated. The other responses are not on point. An in-depth study of available routes would not establish whether the crystals are in danger. Choice B is thus incorrect. The uniqueness of the crystals is not what the Club says will place them in danger. Choice C is thus incorrect. Choice D is incorrect because the existence of an alternate route does not have a bearing on whether the crystals will be destroyed by this freeway. Choice E is also incorrect because an unnecessary freeway does not make it more likely that the crystals will be in danger.

9. *Main Conclusion*

In "main conclusion" questions you must identify the author's unstated main point. To do so you must have a handle on *all* the facts, because they are the source of the main conclusion. It may be helpful to re-read the facts after you have read the answer choices to make sure you use all facts to identify the main point.

Here is a question:

Developed countries have lower trade barriers than developing countries. Developing countries that have become prosperous have lowered barriers to many goods, such as cars and electronic equipment, to expose their industries to foreign competition. Countries should use trade barriers to grow industries to be competitive on a global scale. Then, they should selectively lower their trade barriers. Developed economies can further strengthen their economies by eliminating trade barriers. Increased global commerce is in everyone's best interest.

The author's main point is:

(A) Global commerce helps development.
(B) Trade barriers can serve a useful purpose.
(C) Industries grow faster with government intervention.
(D) Some countries are stronger because they trade more.
(E) Countries should cooperate to stimulate growth through trade.

Choice B is correct because it sums up the author's qualified support of trade barriers. The author does not believe trade barriers are always good for economic development, but does believe they can serve a purpose.

Choice A is wrong because it is too broad. The author believes that certain countries can grow by blocking global commerce through trade barriers. Answer C is wrong because the passage says nothing about the speed of growth. Choice D is incorrect because the passage says nothing about whether the level of trade is connected to a country's strength. Instead, it speaks of the level of countries' trade barriers. The passage discusses how different kinds of countries should use trade barriers differently. It does not establish how, or whether, those countries should coordinate those different trade strategies. Thus, answer E is wrong.

10. *Reasoning*

In reasoning questions you must identify the kind of reasoning in the question. Here is an illustration:

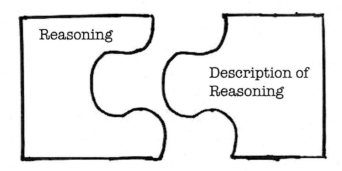

Here is a question:

Store manager: The procedure for stacking shelves is to organize them in a manner that maximizes sales. Store clerks are not following that procedure because they are placing items that do not sell well in prominent shelf spaces.

Store clerk: They are following store procedure because items that do not sell well need to be prominently displayed so that more people will buy them. Customers will buy products that sell well even though they are not prominently displayed on shelves.

The store clerk responds by:

(A) Establishing that the manager, while generally correct, has overlooked a detail.
(B) Demonstrating that the manager's observation does not separate theory from practice.
(C) Arguing that, when penalizing clerks, the motives for the clerks' actions should be taken into account.
(D) Telling the manager that the clerks have a different understanding of the store business than the manager.
(E) Justifying an interpretation of store procedure by calling into question an assumption that the manager made.

A is wrong because the clerk does not point out a detail. B is wrong because both the manager and the clerks are trying to put into practice store procedure. C is incorrect because penalizing the clerks is not an issue in this question. D is correct, but it is not the best answer because it says nothing about the fact that the clerk calls into question an assumption made by the manager. E is thus correct. The clerk argues store procedure is being followed, though in a different manner than what the manager wanted.

11. *Explain*
In "explain" questions, you must identify information that best explains an apparent discrepancy. You must resolve the dilemma. In these questions you will be given a set of facts, followed by conflicting facts. These questions can be illustrated as follows:

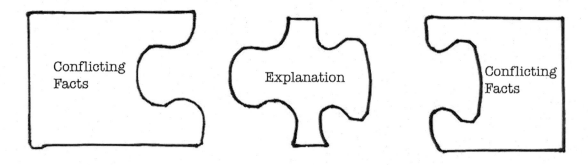

Here is a question:

Students learn best when they are highly motivated, either by their parents, their teachers, athletes or because they have a genetic predisposition to being motivated. At Hector High, students' scores on state exams are below average, even though the students are motivated. In fact, the most motivated students have the lowest scores on those exams at Hector High.

The above situation can be explained by the fact that:

(A) Motivated students can put their energies into things that are not tested on state exams, like sports.
(B) The state exams do not accurately reflect how motivated a test taker is.
(C) Intelligence and dedication are more important to learning than motivation.
(D) Most other schools have students that are even more motivated than those at Hector High.
(E) Motivation is only one factor that determines success on the state exams.

From the stem of the question you know that you are looking for conflicting facts. The dilemma here is found in this sentence "At Hector High, students' scores on state exams are below average, even though the students are motivated." The next sentence accentuates this dilemma: "In fact, the most motivated students have the lowest scores on those exams at Hector High."

Answer choice E is a tempting explanation. It implies that factors other than motivation caused the lower test scores. But, that explanation does not account for the fact that the most motivated students have the lowest test scores. If motivation helped test takers on the exam, then more motivated students should do better in general than other students.

Answer choice A explains why motivated students can do poorly on the exam and is the correct response. The more students are motivated to put their energy into activities not tested on the exam, the worse they will do on the exam. Choice B may look tempting. Test results could be explained by the fact that the exam inaccurately reflects a test taker's motivation. However, choice B does not explain why the most motivated students have the lowest test scores. Furthermore, there is no indication that the tests seek to test motivation in the first place.

C. Structure Your Attack

Here is an outline of how you should attack logical reasoning questions:

1. Do easier and shorter questions first, leave longer and harder questions for later.
2. Answer each question in the following sequence:
   a. Read the stem of the question
   b. Read the facts accompanying each question
   c. Re-read the stem of the question
   d. Depending on what works for you, imagine the correct answer, or go straight to the answer choices

      e.   Grade *all* the answer choices and select your response

3. In one sitting, transfer to the answer sheet answers on each set of pages that face each other.

4. Do lengthy but straightforward questions.

5. Answer difficult questions and double check the accuracy of how you transferred some of the questions you have already answered.

6. If you run out of time, guess on the remaining questions. If you have time left over, double check answers to difficult questions. Then, rest for a few minutes.

You may be thinking: "Wow, that's six steps, one of which has four sub steps! How am I going to remember all those steps!?" After you practice, this sequence will seem natural and become second nature.

Here is how to develop each point of this plan of attack.

1. *Do easier and shorter questions first, leave longer and harder questions for later*

Skip over certain questions that have many words (such as parallel reasoning questions because they take longer to answer. Place a circle around the question number of all questions you skip.

Attack fact patterns with two sets of questions. There is generally less reading per question, so you can get more mileage out of the facts.

You want to spend more time on certain questions that are more difficult for you. For these questions, write a question mark next to the fact pattern. You can then go back and revisit them at the end of the section if you have time.

2. *Answer the questions*

The sequence in which you read these questions is important because it will help you understand *exactly* what the question is asking. Unlike questions that you run across in life in general, LSAT questions are tied specifically to fact patterns that directly affect how you answer the question.

a. Read the stem of the question

First, read the stem of the question, which is the part of the question that actually asks the question. Then, read the question's facts. Then, re-read the question stem. This sequence will help you focus on what part of a question's facts are significant because you first find out what is being asked. However, keep in mind that all facts can have a bearing on determining which answer is correct. In causation questions, for example, the stem of the question will read something like "The author assumes that:"

b. Read the facts accompanying the question

Read the facts with an eye for picking up what is called for in the stem of the question. When you go into the facts you'll get a story that will go something like this:

Farmer Brown used a new fertilizer on his corn field this season. This season that corn field produced a record amount of corn. Therefore, Mr. Brown benefited from the use of the new fertilizer.

Here, there are two elements: the use of a new fertilizer and a record corn crop. The author believes the two are connected, but there is nothing in the passage that establishes a concrete connection. It is possible that there was a record amount of rain or that Mr. Brown used a superior strain of corn. It is also possible that, because of warm weather, the growing season was longer, thereby causing the crop to be larger.

The stem of the question will help you focus on the concept being asked. This will help you filter out a lot of information that is not necessary to answer the question. For example, in the above question the name of the farmer, and of the crop, is completely irrelevant. Instead of farmer Brown, we could be talking about farmer Smith, Jones, or anyone else and the correct answer to the above question would not change. But, if the stem of the question asks you to compare crops of two different farmers, then you would need to pay attention to the names of the farmers and of their crops. Similarly, when you first read this question it is reasonable to conclude that it could be about wheat, beans or any other crop instead of corn and the question would also not change.

Here is the question with all its non-essential information crossed out:

~~Farmer~~ Brown used a new fertilizer ~~on his corn field~~ this season. This season ~~that corn field~~ produced a record ~~amount of corn.~~ Therefore, ~~Mr.~~ Brown benefited from the ~~use of the new~~ fertilizer.

~~The author~~ assumes ~~that:~~

As you practice, you should develop the skill of picking out the key facts, even when there is not a lot of text to begin with. In your initial read, you should focus on only half of the words in the facts and stem above. That is 19 of the 38 words. You should be able to gloss over the 19 crossed out words and understand the question without taking time to absorb them in detail.

The text crossed out above is the result of a judgment about the significance of facts when you first read them. As you progress through the answer choices, sometimes you will find that a certain fact, or the absence of a certain fact, is significant (as you will see, the word "corn" actually is significant for this question). Thus, your understanding of what facts are significant will change, and improve, as you work through some of the questions. This is a good thing because you generally do not have enough time to absorb all the key facts of a question with minute precision on the first pass. Also, without reading all of the answer choices, sometimes you do not have enough information from which to discern the key facts.

For example, as you progress through the record corn harvest question you will find that it is helpful to know that this question is about corn in particular and not about plants in general. Answer choice B reads "The new fertilizer is good for plant growth and makes them produce more." However, in reading through the stem of the question and the facts there is no way for you to know about the corn – plant distinction. You should not spend a lot of time focusing on the stem and the facts to the point where you will not be able to discern that the facts did not say anything about plants. There are an infinite number of things that are not mentioned in the facts. When you get into the answer choices and see that plants are mentioned, you may not remember whether they were listed in the facts. This is especially true if, through your intuition, you filter out a number of words you do not consider significant when you first read the stem and facts. If you can't remember whether the facts said anything about plants, then jump back to the facts and read them with an eye for any mention of plants. When you find that this question is only about corn, and not plants, you will be able to make a more informed decision about eliminating answer choice B.

Additional analysis of answer choice B, and how it relates to the other answer choices, is found below.

c. Re-read the stem of the question

Re-reading the stem of the question is a good idea because it is the most important part of the question. You must understand *exactly* what it is asking. Not only will that determine which facts are significant, it will also determine which response you select. In our example the stem is, again, "The author assumes that:" With practice, you will be able to fully understand this phrase by simply remembering the word "assumes."

d. Depending on what works for you, imagine the correct answer, or go straight to the answer choices

What you do next can vary from person to person, and you should explore what works best for you.

Some test takers find that it is best to imagine the correct answer at this point, before reading the answer choices, because those choices are often designed to trick you. These people find that, if you have an idea of what the answer should be, then you will be better able to find the answer when you read through the answer choices.

However, this approach has its shortfalls. It takes a little time to come up with an answer and that time is expensive. Also, a question may test a specific part of the fact pattern, in which case coming up with a general answer will not be very helpful. Finally, you may come up with a wrong answer. You wouldn't make such a mistake if you didn't try to come up with an answer in the first place. Also, the examiners try to trick you every step of the way by using convoluted facts, in addition to using distracting answer choices.

If it works for you, go straight to the answer choices, identify the best answer and use the process of elimination to eliminate wrong choices.

Use trial and error to determine which method works for you. If you are from the Northeast and have a background similar to people who write the exam and those who do well on it (i.e., people from elite law schools), then you may benefit from imagining an answer before attacking the answer choices. If you are from a background different from that of the test makers and answers do not flow from the facts naturally for you, the process of elimination approach may be best for you.

e. Read and rate *all* the answer choices and select your response

You must look at every answer choice because you are being asked to select the *best* answer. Even if you think you have a good answer, there may be one that is even better, so keep looking through the answers.

Like questions, answers are of varying levels of difficulty. Some answers are obviously right, some are obviously wrong, and some are in between. As you review each answer you should rate it, or give it a grade. Don't take too much time to assign a grade to an answer, simply write down what immediately comes to mind.

This is a critical step because you are being asked to select the best answer. This means you must know the strength of the answer choices relative to each other and select the best one. Your task is especially difficult if you must select from a group of answers that are all wrong or that are all right. For this reason, you need to assign answer choices various levels of "correct" grades and of "failing" grades.

Use the following grading scheme:

Some answer choices appear to be *completely* wrong. Place an "X" through the letter that identifies them, and then place another "X" next to that letter.

Other answer choices appear to be less obviously wrong. Grade these by putting an "X" through the letter that identifies them.

Still other answer choices appear wrong, but not completely wrong. Place one line, like this line: /, through the letter that identifies them.

You may not be sure about some answer choices. Place a question mark ("?") beside them.

An answer choice may appear to be correct, but you're not completely sure. Place one check mark (a "√") beside the letter that identifies it.

Another answer choice may appear to be the clear winner. Place two check marks ("√√") beside the letter that identifies it.

If you've given only one "clear winner" grade to the answer choices and failing grades to the rest of the choices, circle the letter identifying the clear winner and move on to the next question.

If you've given one "clear winner" ("√√") grade and one simple passing grade (a "√"), or if you've given more than one answer choice a passing grade, go back and make sure you think the clear winner is a better answer than the answer that received a simple passing grade. Circle the letter identifying your selection and move on.

Here again is our example, with answer choices:

Farmer Brown used a new fertilizer on his corn field this season. This season that corn field produced a record amount of corn. Therefore, Mr. Brown benefited from the use of the new fertilizer.

The author assumes that:

(A) The author does not assume anything because the fertilizer obviously helped the corn plants produce the record harvest.
(B) The new fertilizer is good for plant growth and makes them produce more.
(C) The new fertilizer was a significant factor, among all plant growth factors, that caused the record corn harvest.
(D) Apart from the use of the fertilizer, farmer Brown did not significantly change the way he farmed his corn crop this year.
(E) The field did not produce a record amount of corn because of factors different from the new fertilizer, such as seed or weather.

Answer choice A is clearly wrong. Correct answer choices do not contradict the stem of the question in this manner. Answer choice B is wrong, but not as clearly wrong. It is wrong for two reasons. One, it is too broad. This question is about corn, not plants in general.

Second, this question is not about whether fertilizer (or the new fertilizer) is good for growth. The issue is narrower. It is whether the *new* fertilizer is what caused the record corn crop.

Answer choice C is less clearly wrong. It is generally correct, but not the best answer. From the facts of the question we have nothing to infer that the author considered a number of growth factors and decided that the new fertilizer was the most significant factor. However, it appears that the author believes the new fertilizer is the only growth factor. As such, it would be the most significant factor. There is, however, a better answer choice.

Answer choice D is an even closer call. If, as the question's facts imply, the new fertilizer was the only significant factor that caused the record crop, then farmer Brown must not have otherwise changed the way he farmed. Thus, answer choice D is probably true. But it is not the best answer. The author's assumption goes beyond assuming something about farmer Brown's farming practices. The author assumes that *nothing* other than the new fertilizer caused the record crop. Thus, the author assumes that "factors different from the new fertilizer" did not cause the record crop. "Different factors" include both farmer Brown's farming practices and other things not in his control, such as the weather and bugs. Answer choice E includes this broader description of the author's assumption and is thus correct.

Not all questions ask you to make this fine a distinction. However, you must be able to detect when answer choices are close like these. That way, you will spend more time on them, re-read the facts, and get to a point where one answer choice makes more sense to you than the rest.

The correct answers do not have to be immediately apparent to you. Think of this as a process. As you read through the answer choices, you become aware that some of the choices are close. If the answer is not clear to you, re-read the facts and the close answers so every single significant word is fresh in your mind. Then, compare each close answer choice to understand exactly how they are different. Eventually, you should find the answer choice that most closely fits the facts.

Here is how the question could look after you have graded all the answer choices:

> Farmer Brown used a new fertilizer on his corn field this season. This season that corn field produced a record amount of corn. Therefore, Mr. Brown benefited from the use of the new fertilizer.
>
> The author assumes that:
>
> ✗ ✗ (A) The author does not assume anything because the fertilizer obviously helped the corn plants produce the record harvest.
> (B) The new fertilizer is good for plant growth and makes them produce more.
> ? (C) The new fertilizer was a significant factor, among all plant growth factors, that caused the record corn harvest.
> (D) Apart from the use of the fertilizer, farmer Brown did not significantly change the way he farmed his corn crop this year.
> (E) The field did not produce a record amount of corn because of factors different from the new fertilizer, such as seed or weather.

If, after you've graded all the answer choices, you have not assigned a single "passing" grade, you may have misread the stem of the question or the facts. Go back and re-read them. But, it is possible that this question may simply ask you to identify the best of five bad answers, in which case that is what you must do. You must make sure you have not misread the question though. When you misread a question you may also find there are no answer choices to answer the question as you understood it.

Grading the answer choices is part of the process of getting to the answer, and you're trying to do it as efficiently as possible. It is ok to go back and assign different grades to answers after you have re-read the facts and question stem. Simply cross out your prior grade and assign the new grade. Don't erase your prior markings because that takes more time.

With practice, you will develop judgment that will help you get a feel for how strong your answer is. If, after grading a difficult question's answer choices, you are still not sure about your answer, place a question mark beside the entire question. Record answers to such questions when you transfer answers in blocks.

If you have time at the end of a section, return to this question once again. The second time around your mind may see things a little differently. You will be more familiar with the problem, but might not be stuck in any ruts you may have been in when you first looked at the question. Sometimes, after re-reading the question, you are able to become more assured of an answer. If that happens, cross out the "?" next to the answer and move on to other questions with question marks next to them.

3. *In one sitting, transfer answers to the answer sheet for each set of pages that face each other*

Transfer all responses for questions that appear on each set of two pages that face each other, regardless of how many questions there are. Don't spend your time trying to figure out whether you're transferring the answers in sets of 6, 7 or 8. Just use this rule of thumb.

As you transfer your answers you must adjust to the fact that you are skipping difficult questions and saving them for later. You should circle the numbers identifying the difficult questions you skip over. When transferring your scores on your initial pass through the logical reasoning section, you should not place any answers for the questions you have skipped over. If you guess by darkening a bubble for these questions, you must later erase it when you come back and answer the question. That will take precious time.

When transferring the questions on the initial pass, make sure you know the number that corresponds for *each answer* you transfer. In other words, don't transfer one answer and then simply transfer the next answer in relation to the first answer you transferred. For example, if your answer to question 3 is "c," your answer to question 4 is "d," and your answer to question 5 is "a," don't transfer your answers quickly by looking at the string of answers as "c, d, a," going to the bubble sheet, inserting "c" at question 3, and then simply inserting "d" and then "a" in the following answer spaces. You are more likely to make a careless mistake if you do so, and those mistakes are just as costly as if you had never read a question and had no idea how to answer it. You will be skipping some questions on this initial pass through (such as the more difficult ones, and the longer ones) so you need to be certain that you're consciously aware of every answer to every question.

However, if you are able to consciously remember the specific question numbers and corresponding answers to sets of three or four questions, then transferring answers in sets is a good idea. Transferring scores in that manner may be faster, and if you can do so without any careless errors, then that is the way to go. To minimize careless errors it might be best to simply transfer answers one at a time, even if it takes you a little more time to do so. Your mind is getting a little rest with this change of pace, so the time is not completely wasted.

4. *Do the lengthy but straightforward questions*

These are questions that are not difficult for you, but have a lot of text with them. Parallel reasoning questions can be lengthy, so here is where you might want to do such questions.

This is like picking fruit that is in the middle of a tree: you know you can reach it, but it will take more effort than the low hanging fruit.

5. *Do the difficult questions and double check the accuracy of how you transferred some of the questions you have already answered*

At this point your brain has been working reasonably hard, and you have eaten through a bunch of time. Now, your brain will have to work harder to answer these difficult questions, and you may not get all of them right. Under these circumstances, it is important that you remain at ease. You are executing a plan that, overall, will get you the most correct answers.

While answering difficult questions, you should check the accuracy with which you transferred previous answers to the answer sheet because your brain must work more on these hard questions. Doublechecking that accuracy is the easiest thing you will do on the exam, and will give your mind a rest while you tackle these difficult questions.

6. *If you run out of time, guess on the remaining questions. If you have time left over, double check answers to difficult questions*

You must spend enough time on difficult questions so that you understand them. You must not seek to have a partial understanding of a hard question, and then "half guess" at the answer. "Half guesses" on questions that are designed to trick you have the same value as a complete guess. In other words, you will probably not increase your likelihood of getting a correct answer by making a "half guess."

When you have about a minute left in the section, make an outright guess on any difficult questions you have not yet answered. Outright guesses are way better than "half guesses" for a number of reasons. You can do them very quickly. You simply pull out your answer sheet and fill out a bubble by any answer that has not yet been answered. You do not have to worry about errors in transferring your answer, and you do not have to read a single word in the question. Best of all, you have a one in five chance of getting an entirely correct response to a tough question answered correctly in a minimal amount of time.

Do not let your mind feel uneasy about guessing. It is simply part of a broader strategy to get as many correct answers as possible.

IV. WAR GAMES

More people improve their performance here than anywhere else.

"War Games" are problem sets that operate like little games. While each game is different, they have many similarities. Many test takers can improve significantly by understanding the genre of these games.

As in a card game where you must use cards in a manner consistent with the rules, you must manipulate war game units according to game rules. The units of the game can be things such as people, houses, or events. The units are organized in a certain manner, such as around a table, along a street, or during a month.

Articulating game rules in pictures and shorthand that can be easily applied to each question is the key to success. Many people can vastly increase their grasp of complex concepts when they visualize them.

If you first do not understand a question, come back to it later in the game and it may be clearer to you. Think of yourself as a mountain climber. A game is the mountain and the answers are resting along a winding path that leads to the top of the mountain. The hardest question is at the mountaintop. The path is the reasoning steps that you must follow to obtain answers. The path is a winding one, and a question may rest on top of a cliff that is too steep for you to climb. When that happens, climb toward a different question. In the process you may see a roundabout path to that question on top of the cliff. Take it!

Let's work on improving your game.

A. The Exam's Directions

Here are the directions on the exam for these games. Read and understand them now and don't read them when you take the exam, because they probably will not change.

> Directions: Each group of questions in this section is based on a set of conditions. In answering some of the questions, it may be useful to draw a rough diagram. Choose the response that most accurately and completely answers each question and blacken the corresponding space on your answer sheet.

These directions should be clarified. First, the sentence "In answering some of the questions, it may be useful to draw a rough diagram" should read "In answering *all* of the questions it *will be useful* to draw a *simple* and *accurate* diagram." For all of these games, you should begin by diagramming the rules (more on this below). A "rough" diagram will not necessarily lead you to the correct answer choice because the questions for these games require that you understand the games with precision.

Second, the sentence "Choose the response that most accurately and completely answers each question and blacken the corresponding space on your answer sheet" should read "Choose the *correct* response for each question and blacken the corresponding space on your answer sheet." Fortunately, games have right and wrong answers. You do not have to choose the best answer. There are no responses that "most accurately and completely" answer a question. Either an answer choice correctly answers a question or it does not.

B. Plan Of Attack

You should attack games in the sequence outlined below. The following techniques will make the games more understandable by simplifying them.

1. *Choose which war games, and which questions, to attack first*

Some war games are more difficult than others. You should identify games that are easiest for you and do those first. As you practice these questions you will get a sense for which games are easier for you. Whether games ask you to schedule events, or organize places geographically, do what is easiest for you first. If a game type does not look familiar to you when you scan over it, leave it for later.

Some games have more questions attached to them than others. You may want to do those games earlier because usually the hardest part of each game is understanding the rules.

Once you understand the rules, it is not as difficult to apply those rules to specific questions. Generally speaking, if there are more questions for a set of rules, you can answer each of those questions more efficiently.

Before you dive into the rules of each game you should scan through all the games and organize them according to which game you will do first. You should organize them according to the criteria described above, and place a number by each game. Then, start reading closely the rules of the game you have identified as #1.

You should complete all questions in a game, no matter how difficult they are, before proceeding to the next set of questions. Unlike logic games, in war games it is more difficult to go back and revisit difficult questions towards the end of the 35 minute period. The set of rules for each game will not be fresh in your mind at the end of the period.

Not only are certain war games harder than others, within each war game certain questions are harder than others. You must be sure to answer the easier questions correctly, and have a strategy for answering the harder questions. Easier questions in a game will help answer the more difficult questions by familiarizing you with the rules.

War games usually have a finite number of possible arrangements of their units. For example, there are only so many ways a set of people can be seated around a table. Sometimes you must know the entire universe of possible unit sequences to correctly answer a question. For example, you could have a question that goes like this: "What is the total number of possible seating arrangements under the rules for seating people around the table?" Those are the harder questions.

To understand a game's universe of possibilities you must understand and apply all the rules, and possibly all the rules that can be deduced from the game's facts. The longer you work with a particular game, the better you will understand its rules. You will be able to manipulate the units within that game with more ease. When you have a better understanding of the rules, you can go back and answer the harder questions.

Hard questions take more time to answer. You should develop the judgment to know about how much time you can spend. Ideally, these questions will appear in the last game and you will answer them last.

2. *Write the game's units, in groups if necessary*

First, write out all the game's units. Here is an example of units: "The following sporting events may be scheduled in one week: soccer, sailing, volleyball and baseball. These concerts may also be scheduled: Jazz, Rock and Roll, Rap, and Hip Hop."

Each unit should be represented by a letter, which should be the first letter of the unit's name. Don't write the full name of units, such as "soccer," because it takes more time to both write and read the entire word. It is best to think of that unit simply as "s" rather than as "soccer." The fact that the unit is "soccer", by itself, will probably not have a bearing on selecting an answer.

As you read the list of units, make sure none of them begin with the same first letter. The examiners can get tricky and assign two or more units names that begin with the same letter. If they do this, you must symbolize these units with two or more letters to distinguish them. In our example, you should use "so" to represent soccer and "sa" to represent sailing. You cannot simply use "s" because you will then confuse soccer with sailing.

If the units are in two or more groups, select symbols that distinguish each group and organize the units into groups. The most effective way to do so is to use upper and lower case letters. Organize the units in a manner that is most natural to you and place a label above each group of letters. Thus, in our example we have

sports | concerts
Sa, So, W, b | J, RR, R, H

This will serve as a quick reference when you are in the thick of a question. It allows you to see in an instant the universe of eight units and their organization. Placing a circle around these letters will help distinguish them from other writings on your exam. With practice you may find you do not need to circle these notes.

You may think to yourself "I don't need to write this out because I can tell Rap is a concert and not a sport." But, it is easiest to manipulate these units by using only letters. These notes are a helpful reference because you may not think of "RR" as being a concert simply by looking at the letters.

Placing units in groups is also useful because the differences between the groups may not always be as obvious as sports and concerts. For example, you could have one category of African animals and another of South American animals.

3. *Write the structure for the units*

Next, write out the places into which the units will be organized. For our example, write the following letters and grid:

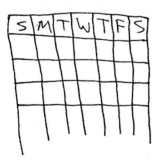

S M T W T F S

By simply looking at the sequence of letters "S M T W T F S" it should be clear to you that they represent days of the week. If the game rules indicate that events can be held in the morning or afternoon on any given day, then draw a line down the middle of the column for each day. You shouldn't have to label each column "Morning" and "Evening" because those columns follow chronologically as do the columns for each day of the week.

The grid should be expandable for each question in the game. Find a place on the exam booklet with enough space so that you can extend the grid as necessary. Otherwise, you will have to draw another grid. That will take time. The more times you draw the grid, the more likely you are to make a mistake.

If a question asks you to seat people around the table, draw lines like this:

The above table seats eight people.

Your task is to simplify the game by making it abstract. You can also simplify the game by organizing it in a manner that is intuitive for you. For example, in a spatial game, North is always up.

4. *Draw the game's rules*

You should draw rules because doing so helps you understand and remember them. Most importantly, the drawing serves as a quick reference tool.

This is the hardest and most important step in war games. It's hard because complicated rules can require the use of a combination of logic symbols, words and pictures.

This step is important because you must follow game rules with precision to identify correct responses. It is critical that you accurately draw rules because the drawings will become *the* reference for your analysis. Generally, you should not have to go back and re-read rules in their fully written out text form.

If you cannot identify a correct response by looking at your rule drawings, then you will need to go back and re-read the rules. You may find your shorthand of the rule was not accurate, or that it did not fully reflect what the rule says. Your rule drawings should be accurate enough for this not to happen regularly. However, you also do not want to spend an inordinate amount of time drawing rules and refining your drawings so that you run out of time. Test takers generally err on the side of not spending enough time drawing rules with care. So, you may want to begin your studies by drawing rules with extra care and then speeding up the pace from there. You can find a point at which your drawings, for the most part do the job; and where they don't, you will be able to quickly adjust by re-reading rules and moving forward.

Here again are the facts of our example, followed by game rules:

> The following sporting events may be scheduled
> in one week: soccer, sailing, volleyball and baseball.
> These concerts may also be scheduled: Jazz, Rock
> and Roll, Rap, and Hip Hop.
>> The events occur as follows:
>> Soccer is scheduled on Friday.
>> Each event may be scheduled only once.
>> Jazz must be scheduled after volleyball.
>> Baseball must be played before volleyball.
>> If Hip Hop is scheduled, then sailing is also
>>> scheduled.
>> Volleyball must be scheduled.
>> If sailing is scheduled then Rock and Roll is
>>> scheduled on Tuesday.

As you read through the facts you should focus on words and letters that are not crossed out below:

~~The following sporting~~ events may be
~~scheduled in one~~ week: s~~occer~~, sa~~iling~~, v~~olleyball~~
and b~~aseball~~. ~~These~~ concerts may ~~also~~ be
scheduled: J~~azz~~, R~~ock and Roll~~, R~~ap~~, and H~~ip Hop~~
~~The events occur as follows:~~
    So~~ccer~~ is ~~scheduled on~~ Friday.
    ~~Each event may be scheduled only once.~~
    J~~azz must be scheduled~~ after v~~olleyball~~.
    B~~aseball~~ must be ~~played~~ before v~~olleyball~~.
    If H~~ip Hop is scheduled~~ then sa~~iling is also~~
~~scheduled~~.
    V~~olleyball~~ must be scheduled.
    If sa~~iling is scheduled~~ then R~~ock and Roll is~~
~~scheduled~~ on Tuesday.

Games have less text than other sections of the exam, so your eyes can rest. In fact, notice how many parts of the text have no bearing on your task of choosing the right answer. You do not have to keep a lot of text fresh in your mind. You must, however, reason well with the information that is significant.

Only the first letters of the game's units are not crossed out. You should think of units as simply letters when you first read the game's facts.

Generally, do not focus on rules that tell you a unit may be used only once because you instinctively should plan to use units only once. However, you generally should diagram that rule because it could conceivably come into play. Questions that require you to know the entire universe of unit sequences necessarily require you to know all the rules. For such questions, you can mentally check off the use of each unit and each rule by looking at your drawings of each unit and each rule.

More advanced test takers may consider not drawing rules that indicate units are used only once.

a. Write rules in a structure

Draw any rules that fit into the game structure. Here, only the first rule fits. Write game rule for "Soccer is scheduled on Friday" as:

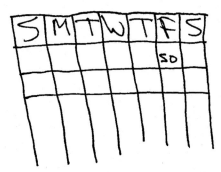

b. Write deductions

As you write rules it is helpful to write deductions from those rules. From this rule we can deduce that soccer will not be played on other days. Generally, deductions should not be placed on the same row however or same area as a rule. This is because sometimes a question will ask you to change a rule. If that happens, you do not want to be confused by deductions based on rules that are not valid for a question.

We illustrate the deduction that soccer is not played on days other than Friday like this:

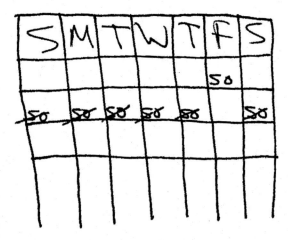

This deduction takes a fair amount of time to write because it fills in many days. A more advanced method is to not write out these lengthy deductions. If you can do so accurately, just make a mental note of them as you diagram the rules.

You want to write this deduction small in each box to leave room for other deductions that may arise.

You should write out any deductions that are immediately apparent to you, but don't spend too much time. You can make more deductions later for individual questions as necessary. It is possible that you will not have to use each deduction you come up with, in which case you don't want to have spent the time making such deductions. However, some deductions are so useful that they will enable you to immediately answer a question. Thus, if you see a deduction after a brief review of the rules in the beginning, write it into the grid's second row.

Next to the grid, write rules that do not fit into it.

c. Write rules in shorthand

If a rule cannot be readily drawn, briefly write it. In our scheduling example, for the rule "Each event may be scheduled only once" write:

ea event only once

This does not significantly abbreviate the rule, but is still helpful. You also benefit because, as you write the rule, you are reminded of what it says and thus remember it better.

d. Establish unit order

Establish the order of the units by placing a hyphen between them. Thus, "Jazz is always scheduled after volleyball" is

Conversely, "Baseball must be played before volleyball" is

Notice that from these two rules we can deduce

and

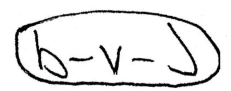

If "b" is before "v" and "v" is always before "J", then "b" must also be before "J". The negatives of these relationships can also deduced as:

  and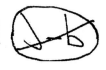

Think of the hyphen as a string that can be extended indefinitely to accommodate as many intervening units as necessary. Be careful that you do not interpret these rules as "Baseball is scheduled *right before* volleyball," because that is not correct. You must interpret the rules to mean exactly what they say. A tricky rule can read "Jazz is scheduled after volleyball." This does not mean that Jazz is scheduled on the day following volleyball if there are less than seven events to be scheduled during a seven day week. It is possible that volleyball is scheduled on Wednesday, nothing is scheduled for Thursday, soccer is on Friday, and Jazz is scheduled for Saturday.

The hyphen should also be used to describe spatial relationships. The rule "Hamlet is west of Sitton" should be diagrammed as:

The hyphen can also be used vertically. Where units are organized on various floor levels a rule could read "Sally lives on a floor that is above Vanessa's floor." This rule would be written:

e. Establish positives

You should illustrate positive relationships by placing units together. For example, if a rule says "Harry and Sally always ride in the car together" you should illustrate that by indicating:

If a rule says Sally and Harry sometimes ride together, then write:

If the rule is that "Harry and Sally never ride together," you should write:

You should cross out mistakes instead of erasing them because crossing out mistakes is faster. But, you should not cross out mistakes in a manner that can be confused with a negative. Thus, if you mistakenly wrote:

cross it out by scribbling on it like this:

f. Contrapositives

Sometimes a unit's presence will always cause the presence of another unit. You should describe this relationship with a "→". Here, "If Hip Hop is scheduled, then sailing is also scheduled" is:

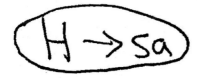

Do not confuse this to mean that sailing is scheduled after Hip Hop. The "→" symbol is different from the hyphen in that it only indicates that the presence of one unit will cause the presence of another unit. The arrow is a symbol for the word "then". The phrase "if Hip Hop occurs then sailing must also occur" becomes simply "H → sa". The shorthand expression of the concept is a *lot* faster than spelling it.

From this relationship we can deduce that, if sailing is not scheduled, then Hip Hop must also not be scheduled. This deduction is called a "contrapositive." The shorthand for it is:

This kind of deduction is not intuitive for some people, so it may be a good idea to simply memorize it.

Note that this is not a valid deduction: sa → H. If sailing is scheduled, Hip Hop may, but does not necessarily have to be, scheduled.

g. When units go in different places

Even though units generally are used once, often they may be placed in more than one place. This should be symbolized with arrows connecting the letter for such unit to the places where the it may be placed. In our example, if there were a rule that said "Volleyball may be scheduled only on Sunday or Monday" it would be diagrammed as:

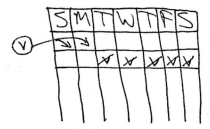

5. *Advanced Method: Rules You Do Not Diagram*

You should develop a series of default rules which, if they appear in a question, are so obvious to you that you will not have to diagram them. These are usually simple and general rules such as, "Each event is scheduled only once during the week" and "Only one event is scheduled on a given day." This last rule can be diagramed by drawing a grid with boxes that can fit only one letter. If more than one event can be scheduled in a day, then you should create enough boxes under each day for each slot that can be scheduled.

As you practice you should develop a sense for which other kinds of rules are intuitive for you. If a rule is not intuitive, you should diagram it to make sure you follow it. Towards the end of this war games section is an example of advanced diagramming of rules. It does not have all the diagramming described above because advanced test takers do not need to diagram as much.

6. *Answer the questions*

Questions that ask you to assume that a basic rule has changed should be left for later. They require that you understand both what the rule was and the implications of changing that rule. When you move on to further questions, you must not apply the changed rule unless you are told to do so. Questions that require you to apply many game rules should also be left for later because they are usually more complicated.

After you have diagrammed rules and deductions, some question answers will automatically flow. In our scheduling example we have these diagrams, which are divided between rules and deductions. The deductions are on the third row of the grid and in the second column of diagrams by the grid. The division should be intuitive, so you shouldn't label which diagrams are for rules and which are for deductions.

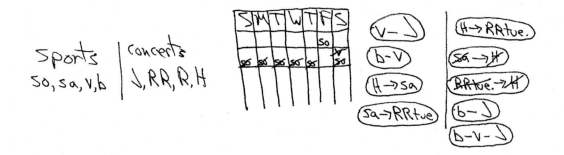

a. Write units and deductions until you find the answer
Here is a question:

1. If Hip Hop is scheduled on Monday, which of the
following must be true:

(A) Sailing is scheduled on Tuesday.
(B) Rap is not scheduled.
(C) Baseball is on Thursday.
(D) Jazz is on Saturday.
(E) Soccer is on Thursday.

One of the most important words in this question is "must". Some of the responses may be true, but you need the response that *has to be true*.

Here is a grid with the question's rule and its deductions. Place a "1" next to the row for this question in case you want to look back and double check your work. That will indicate that this is the row for question number one.

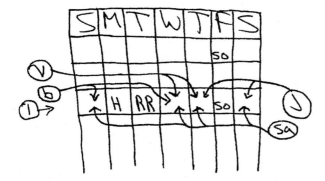

You first plot the events you know with certainty. Here, we know Hip Hop and soccer are on Monday and Friday respectively. We also know that, because Hip Hop is scheduled, sailing must also be scheduled. Because sailing is scheduled, Rock & Roll must be on Tuesday.

From the b – v – J deduction we can place each one of those letters in either of two places. Sailing must occur on any of the free days.

The relationships in this question may seem complicated, but they are substantially more understandable when they are visualized. More deductions could be plotted, but would not be helpful here. For example, for Sunday you could plot the absence of "J" and "v". Knowing when to stop diagramming is a matter of judgment.

If you finish diagramming and are unable to identify the correct response, you may need to either double check your work or draw more deductions. If that happens, do not let it affect your concentration in the least bit. Simply go back, and double check your work. If your work is fine, then make more deductions. If you are still unable to answer the question, mark your best guess, put a question mark next to the question and move on. After you are finished with all the questions for the game, you can revisit this question and triple check your work.

Now we check each question.

A. Sailing cannot be on Tuesday because Rock & Roll must be on Tuesday.

B.   This is the correct answer. Rap cannot be scheduled because the week is full with seven other events.

C.   Baseball can only be on Sunday or Wednesday.

D.   Jazz may be on either Thursday or Saturday.

E.   Soccer must be on Friday.

Here is another question:

2. If all the days have an event and a concert cannot be scheduled right after another concert, all of the following must be true EXCEPT:

(A) At least two sports must be scheduled consecutively.

(B) Volleyball may be scheduled before or after Rock & Roll.

(C) Hip Hop and Rap can both be scheduled.

(D) Jazz cannot be held on Wednesday.

(E) A sport may occur on Thursday.

You learn more about games as you go through them. Initially, you may not have considered the possibility that some days may not have an event. Here, the question flags that issue by telling you that, for this question, all days have an event.

The rule for this question can be diagrammed as follows:

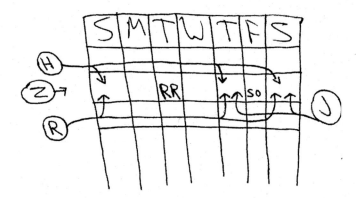

We know there must be four sport events and three concerts because there is not enough room for all the events if all four concerts are held. If Hip Hop is held, then sailing and Rock & Roll must also be held. Because the other three sport events must also be held, that would add up to eight events.

Because there must be four sporting events, we know sailing must be scheduled. Thus, Rock & Roll must be scheduled on Tuesday. Jazz must follow at least two events, but cannot be next to Rock & Roll. Thus, Jazz will be on either Thursday or Saturday. Hip Hop and Rap can be scheduled on any day that is not next to Rock & Roll and that is not occupied by Jazz. More deductions could be made, but this is as far as you should go.

If you are unable to make deductions, move on to a question that appears easier and work on it. Then come back to the difficult question.

Here is an analysis of the answers:

A.   This is true because all four sports must be scheduled and soccer is on Friday. Both Sunday and Monday or both Wednesday and Thursday must have a sport.

B.   Volleyball may occur on Monday, Wednesday or Thursday.

C.   If Hip Hop is scheduled, then sailing must be scheduled, which leaves no room for Rap. If Rap is scheduled, there is not enough room for both Hip Hop and sailing. Thus, this is the correct answer.

D.   Jazz cannot be held on Wednesday because it would be next to Rock & Roll.

E.   If either Hip Hop or Rap are held on Sunday, then a sport must occur on Thursday. But, either Hip Hop or Rap may also occur on Thursday.

Here is another question:

3. If Jazz is scheduled on Tuesday, then:

(A) Hip Hop may not be scheduled.
(B) Sailing may be scheduled on Wednesday.
(C) Baseball is held on Monday.
(D) Six events may be scheduled.
(E) Only four events may be scheduled.

This question looks easier than the prior two questions because the stem of the question is simpler. You should do these kinds of questions first. Here is how the rule and deductions for this question can be diagrammed:

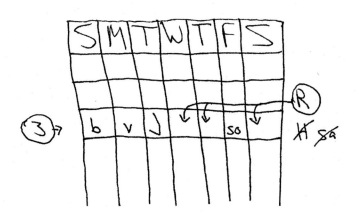

We know "b" and "v" must go before "J", so we write them in. We also know that if Hip Hop is scheduled, sailing must also be scheduled and Rock & Roll must be scheduled on Tuesday. That is not possible because Jazz is on Tuesday. Thus, neither Hip Hop, sailing or Rock & Roll may be scheduled. Rap may be scheduled during any of the open days, but does not have to be scheduled.

Here is an analysis of the answers:

A.   This answer is correct. If Hip Hop is scheduled, Rock & Roll would conflict with Jazz on Tuesday.

B.   If sailing is scheduled, Rock & Roll would also conflict with Jazz.

C.   Baseball must be held on Tuesday.

D & E.   These are incorrect because four or five events may be scheduled.

Here is the next question:

4. Which of the following is an acceptable
continuous sequence of events for a portion of the
week:

(A) Hip Hop, Rock & Roll, soccer.
(B) Baseball, sailing, soccer.
(C) Rap, Hip Hop, Jazz.
(D) Baseball, volleyball, Hip Hop.
(E) Rock & Roll, Jazz, sailing.

Here no additional diagramming is necessary. Thus, it is one of the easier questions that
should be done towards the beginning. You must answer this question by testing each
response against the rules and deductions. Four of the responses will break at least one rule
or deduction. The correct response will remain.

Here is an analysis of the answer choices:

A.   If Hip Hop is scheduled, then Rock & Roll must be on Tuesday. They cannot be next
to soccer, which is on Friday.

B.   These events would not allow for volleyball and Jazz to be scheduled appropriately.
Soccer must be scheduled on Friday. Thus, in this sequence baseball and sailing must be on
Wednesday and Thursday respectively. Volleyball and Jazz must both be scheduled after
baseball, but only Saturday remains open. Thus, these three events cannot be scheduled
sequentially.

C.   Rap and Hip Hop cannot both be scheduled because they would require the use of all
eight events. Also, the events would conflict with Rock & Roll for the Tuesday slot.

D.   The events would conflict with Rock & Roll for the Tuesday slot.

E.   These can be scheduled on Tuesday, Wednesday and Thursday. Thus, this is the
correct response.

Here's the next question:

5. If sailing is not scheduled and Rap is scheduled on
the day following Jazz, then which of the following is
true?

(A) Hip Hop is scheduled on Monday.
(B) Baseball may be scheduled on Tuesday.
(C) Rock & Roll may not be scheduled on Tuesday.
(D) Soccer must be the last scheduled event.
(E) The Rap concert must be held on either
      Wednesday or Thursday.

These rules can be diagramed as:

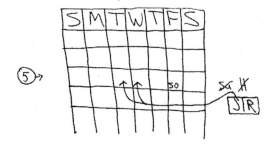

Here are the explanations for this question:

A. If sailing is not scheduled, then Hip Hop also will not be scheduled.
B. Baseball must be scheduled on Sunday or Monday.
C. Rock & Roll may be scheduled on any day except Friday.
D. Soccer *may* be the last scheduled event. Rock & Roll could also be the last event. Thus, D is incorrect.
E. Rap must be held on one of these days because baseball, volleyball and Jazz must be scheduled before Rap. Thus, this is the correct response.

Here is another question:

6. If Jazz and Hip Hop must be scheduled on consecutive days, all of the following must be true EXCEPT:

(A) Rap cannot be scheduled.
(B) Baseball must be held on Monday.
(C) Soccer must be held after Hip Hop.
(D) Rock & Roll must follow volleyball.
(E) Six or seven events may be scheduled.

Here is the diagram:

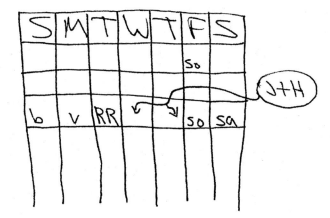

A is wrong because the week is full without Rap. B, C and D are incorrect for reasons that appear on the grid above. Also from the grid above you can see that E is the correct answer. Seven events *must* be scheduled.

Here is the final question for this game:

7. If Jazz must occur the day before Hip Hop, but not necessarily after volleyball, then:

(A) Baseball must occur on Sunday or Wednesday.
(B) Sailing may be scheduled next to Jazz.
(C) Baseball may be held on Thursday.
(D) Sailing may not be scheduled next to baseball.
(E) Rock & Roll must be scheduled before Hip Hop.

Here is the diagram:

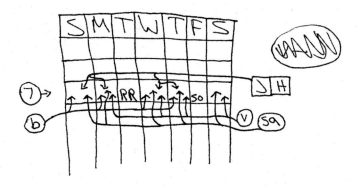

Here a rule becomes invalid. You depict that by scribbling out the rule and deductions from it (see the scribbled out rule to the right above). These questions should be saved for last. You want to have the rule written out and used for other questions. It is also easier to change the rule only once and not change it back to what it was. You lessen the chances you will confuse the rule and its deductions.

Because baseball no longer must be scheduled before Jazz, it can be scheduled on Thursday (if Jazz and Hip Hop are scheduled on Sunday and Monday respectively). Baseball just has to be before volleyball, which can go on Saturday. Thus, answer A is wrong and answer C is correct.

B is wrong because Jazz may only be scheduled next to Hip Hop and Rock & Roll. Jazz may only be scheduled on Sunday or Wednesday. When it is scheduled on Sunday, only Hip Hop is scheduled next to it. If it is on Wednesday, then it is between Hip Hop and Rock & Roll.

D is incorrect because, if sailing is scheduled on either Sunday or Monday, or on either Wednesday or Thursday, it can be scheduled next to baseball. E is incorrect because Hip Hop may be scheduled on Monday.

Check your answers when you finish answering the questions for a particular game. That is a better time than at the end of the entire section because rules are fresher in your mind.

b. Advanced Method: Do not use process of elimination

If your accuracy on these questions is high enough, you should consider not using process of elimination. Once you get the right answer, simply move to the next question. This will save time and allow you to focus on harder questions where you may want to use the process of elimination. Your decision to not use process of elimination should be based on your report card. If you do not get many questions wrong for careless reasons, and yet have difficulty completing this section in the time allotted, then you should definitely consider not using process of elimination on the easier questions. However, if you do not have any time pressure, then you may consider doing process of elimination on some of the questions simply to double check your work.

c. Advanced Method: Do not write out the conditions for each question

With practice, you may reach a point where you are able to visualize the placement of elements without writing them out. If you can, you should use that method to answer the questions. Not only does it save time because you do not have to write out even the letters for the elements, but it also saves space. You don't use up the limited diagramming space in the exam booklet.

You can push yourself by not writing units and see if your number of careless errors goes up. If those errors do not go up, then you can dispense with writing down some units.

d. Advanced diagramming

On the next page is advanced diagramming for the scheduling game we just went through.

The following sporting events may be scheduled in one week: soccer, sailing, volleyball and baseball. These concerts may also be scheduled: Jazz, Rock and Roll, Rap, and Hip Hop. The events occur as follows:

Soccer is scheduled on Friday.

Each event may be scheduled only once.

Jazz must be scheduled after volleyball.

Baseball must be played before volleyball.

If Hip Hop is scheduled, then sailing is also scheduled.

Volleyball must be scheduled.

If sailing is scheduled then Rock and Roll is scheduled on Tuesday.

1. If Hip Hop is scheduled on Monday, which of the following must be true:

   (A) Sailing is scheduled on Tuesday.
   (B) Rap is not scheduled.
   (C) Baseball is on Thursday.
   (D) Jazz is on Saturday.
   (E) Soccer is on Thursday.

2. If all the days have an event and a concert cannot be scheduled right after another concert, all of the following must be true EXCEPT:

   (A) At least two sports must be scheduled consecutively.
   (B) Volleyball may be scheduled before or after Rock & Roll.
   (C) Hip Hop and Rap can both be scheduled.
   (D) Jazz cannot be held on Wednesday.
   (E) A sport may occur on Thursday.

3. If Jazz is scheduled on Tuesday, then:

   So, sa, v, b || J, RR, R, H

   (A) Hip Hop may not be scheduled.
   (B) Sailing may be scheduled on Wednesday.
   (C) Baseball is held on Monday.
   (D) Six events may be scheduled.
   (E) Only four events may be scheduled.

4. Which of the following is an acceptable continuous sequence of events for a portion of the week:

   (A) Hip Hop, Rock & Roll, soccer.
   (B) Baseball, sailing, soccer.
   (C) Rap, Hip Hop, Jazz.
   (D) Baseball, volleyball, Hip Hop.
   (E) Rock & Roll, Jazz, sailing.

5. If sailing is not scheduled and Rap is scheduled on the day following Jazz, then which of the following is true?

   (A) Hip Hop is scheduled on Monday.
   (B) Baseball may be scheduled on Tuesday.
   (C) Rock & Roll may not be scheduled on Tuesday.
   (D) Soccer must be the last scheduled event.
   (E) The Rap concert must be held on either Wednesday or Thursday.

6. If Jazz and Hip Hop must be scheduled on consecutive days, all of the following must be true EXCEPT:

   (A) Rap cannot be scheduled.
   (B) Baseball must be held on Monday.
   (C) Soccer must be held after Hip Hop.
   (D) Rock & Roll must follow volleyball.
   (E) Six or seven events may be scheduled.

7. If Jazz must occur the day before Hip Hop, but not necessarily after volleyball, then:

   (A) Baseball must occur on Sunday or Wednesday.
   (B) Sailing may be scheduled next to Jazz.
   (C) Baseball may be held on Thursday.
   (D) Sailing may not be scheduled next to baseball.
   (E) Rock & Roll must be scheduled before Hip Hop.

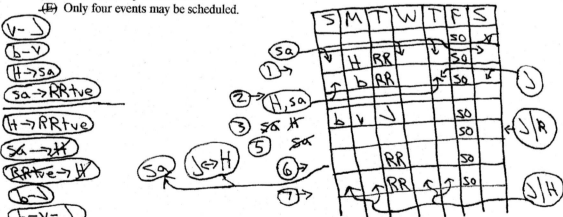

54

Note that this diagram does not show any inaccurate answers and all the diagramming is correct. This will not necessarily occur on the exam. But, remember, you do not have to diagram perfectly to do well! Here is an example of imperfect diagramming that will nonetheless get you the right answer.

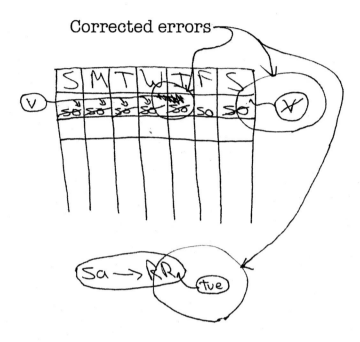

Notice how the circled diagramming areas are corrected. You should develop your own way of correcting your diagramming. It should be intuitive for you and not confuse you. Remember, don't let this affect your morale in the least bit!

7. *Transfer your answers from the booklet to the answer sheet*
This technique is described in the prior section on logical reasoning.

C. Look for Patterns of Wrong Answers
People can usually improve on war games by identifying a certain pattern of problem they encounter and developing a method for diagramming that addresses that problem. Sometimes a certain kind of rule will create problems; or other times, it may be the need to get a handle on the universe of possibilities. So, be on the lookout for patterns of wrong answers. Focus on correcting them.

V. READING COMPREHENSION – POSSIBLY THE ROUGHEST PART OF YOUR JOURNEY
This section is often the most difficult. You are presented with a large amount of dense, technical text on topics that may not be of interest to you. If the topics are of interest to you, don't ponder them because that will just take time away from your task of selecting the accredited responses.

Students usually improve on this section less than on other sections, so you probably want to make other sections a higher priority in your studies. This section is only one-fourth of the exam, and there is not a lot of crossover between the skills for this part and the rest of the exam. There is however, more crossover between war games and logical reasoning. Thus, focusing on improving your skills in those sections will generally help you more than focusing on the reading comprehension section. Because all points on the exam are counted equally, it doesn't matter on which part you pick up points.

Among other things, the reading comprehension section tests your knowledge of the English language. Improving your English proficiency for the sake of the exam is not easy. However, if this section is a real struggle for you because you are a foreign student, you may want to take a year or so to improve your English ability.

A. The Exam's Directions

Here are the exam's directions. Read and understand them now and don't read them when you take the exam, because they probably will not change.

> Directions: Each passage in this section is followed by a group of questions to be answered on the basis of what is <u>stated</u> or <u>implied</u> in the passage. For some of the questions, more than one of the choices could conceivably answer the question. However, you are to choose the <u>best</u> answer; that is, the response that most accurately and completely answers the question, and blacken the corresponding space on your answer sheet.

These directions highlight the largest difficulty with this section: there are no clear-cut right and wrong answers. You must select the best one. The criteria for that selection can be more subjective here than on the rest of the exam.

B. Plan of Attack

You should follow the following sequence when attacking the reading sections:

1. *Do the easier sections first*

Evaluate each of the four passages from first to last, and as you evaluate them place a number from one to four at the top of each passage. The number you place on a passage will be the result of a judgment call based on the factors discussed below. This is not a scientific numbering, with a definite "right" and "wrong" ordering. You do not need to keep close track of exactly what numbers you have placed on all the passages. If you rank two passages as "three" then simply look for a reason for doing one before the other, or just do them one after the other.

Passages on subjects you are familiar with are generally easier to read. For example, if you are an English major and a passage discusses a form of literature, that passage may be easier for you than other passages.

Passages with less text, or with more questions that relate to the text, are also generally easier. You have less information to sift through.

You should also glance over the stems of questions for words that might be red flags for you. For example, if a passage has many general questions that relate to the theme, mood, or tone of the passage you may want to leave that section for last.

2. *Before reading a passage, read the stems of the questions (and not the answer choices) in the section*

This will help you focus on key words and concepts in the passage.

3. *Actively read the passage, focusing on key words and theme*

Underline words or phrases that relate to the stems of the questions. Words that relate to the authors' perspectives or to the main point of the passage will usually have a bearing on at least one question.

Often, questions will ask you to make inferences from the passage, or to arrive at conclusions based on information in the passage. The most common type of question will relate to the main point of the passage, or to what its author would most likely agree with. Other common question types will ask you similar questions about people or positions described in the passage. Some questions will ask about specific facts in the passage, but for the most part you will need to look at clues in the passage that help you arrive at conclusions about the authors' views and other general matters relating to the passage.

Do not focus on highly technical words that you do not completely understand, such as perhaps "chlorofluorocarbons." Their precise meaning usually will not have a bearing on selecting the correct response. However, if a question specifically asks you something that involves the meaning of one such word, you can go back and re-read that word and its surrounding sentences.

Unlike the rest of the exam, you cannot disregard many words in the passage. Here, words throughout the passages have a bearing on its main point, theme, or purpose. You can however, focus on parts of questions. The reading comprehension passage below is reproduced at the end of this reading section with markings that reflect what you should focus on.

4. *Attack the easiest questions first*

Easier questions usually ask you a specific fact about a specific paragraph in the passage. Those kinds of questions are more "cut and dry" than questions that ask you about the mood of the entire passage. After you have spent time answering those specific questions, you will have a better handle on the details of the passage. You are then more able to make general conclusions about the passage.

Once you have decided which questions to answer, grade the answer choices in the same way you grade answer choices on the rest of the exam.

C. A Reading Passage

Here is a passage. You may find it helpful to apply the exam techniques above to the passage and answer the questions. Then, look at the end of this reading comprehension section where the passage is reproduced with markings that reflect the above exam techniques.

The unity of the United States is what has made it so powerful over its history. Professor Gordon has studied this phenomenon and has developed a "unity quotient". To arrive at this quotient, Professor Gordon studied a number of factors that relate to political unity in a country. One important factor is the location of power in a society. Certain societies have a lot of power concentrated in the hands of a few people. In others, power is dispersed throughout the population.

Another factor affecting unity is the number of what Professor Gordon calls "power points" in a society. Those points can be either a person who is a leader, or an ideology that people follow. Power points can collide in a society, and sometimes that is beneficial. For example, in China in the 1980s Deng Xiaopeng was a person who represented a major power point in that country. He advocated free market reforms that were contrary to the communist ideology of China. The result of this collision of power points was economic growth within a framework of political stability. More often, the results of those collisions are civil wars.

A third unity factor is the distance between power points. The further the distance between power points, the less unity exists in a country. Israel is a country with perhaps the biggest distance between power points. Some of its residents, which include radical elements of its Arab population, advocate the destruction of the country. Orthodox Jews on the other hand, view the country as an institution established by God.

The United States has almost an ideal alignment of unity factors. While there is a large political spectrum in the United States, few citizens share the views that represent the ends of the spectrum. For example, the Communist Party exists in the United States, but does not have many members. The vast majority of political power is spread throughout a huge midsection of American voters. By far the biggest issue for those voters is economic prosperity. That is perhaps the biggest power point in American society, and there is not a lot of debate about how to achieve such prosperity. Almost all debate centers on how to spend the less than 10 percent of the budget that relates to welfare, highways, and other miscellaneous matters.

Real tension, leading to disunity, has arisen only once in the history of the United States. The Civil War occurred because power groups in different regions of the country had a fundamentally different approach to achieving the ideal of economic prosperity. For the South, such prosperity would be achieved through the free labor of slaves. For the North, prosperity would be achieved through innovative industries that would hire workers in the labor market. After the War, many African Americans seized hold of that ideal by moving to the north to work in factories. Southern industries have also seized hold of innovation, making the region one of the most vibrant areas of the country.

1. The passage's main point can best be expressed as:

(A) No other country in the history of the world has been as unified as the United States.
(B) A nation's level of unity can be understood by studying a number of factors.
(C) Economic power is best achieved with a high level of unity.
(D) The world's problems can be solved more effectively through a unified approach.
(E) A large number of power points can nonetheless be tightly unified.

2. According to the information presented in the passage about the interplay between unity and power:

(A) The most powerful power point will always prevail against other power points.
(B) Beliefs are usually not as powerful as people in a society.
(C) Chinese society handled internal tension in a manner that increased its power.
(D) The United States will most likely continue to increase its power because it remains unified.
(E) If not properly managed, conflict in Israel could tear the country apart.

GO ON TO THE NEXT PAGE.

3. Based on the information in the passage, Professor Gordon believes:

(A) Politicians would be able to better govern their countries if they understood unity and how to favorably influence the factors that go into the analysis of how unified a society is.
(B) Wars could be avoided if neighboring countries understood the makeup of power in each other and worked toward a constructive resolution to issues that divide them.
(C) Conflict is less likely if power in a society is highly dispersed among a group of people that are towards the middle of the political spectrum of a country.
(D) There has not been a power point as strong as the belief in economic prosperity in the United States among most citizens.
(E) It is possible to assemble different kinds of data into a numerical value that can provide a meaningful comparison of a level of unity that exists in societies at a given point in time.

4. According to the information provided in the passage, a country is probably most unified if:

(A) it can exercise its power on other countries effectively
(B) most of its people adhere to most of the same beliefs
(C) many of its people share significant priorities
(D) it does not have a wide political spectrum with vastly different views
(E) most of its citizens have the spirit of cooperation to overcome differences

5. The passage most supports which of the following statements about "power points" in a society?

(A) They are a significant factor that affects the analysis of how unified a country is.
(B) Significant power points are different in every country.
(C) They are largely beyond the control of any single person.
(D) Most people are unaware of how influential these points are.
(E) They are often destructive because they usually compete with each other.

6. The function of the second to the last paragraph is most likely to:

(A) establish how the United States is superior to other countries in its form of social organization
(B) show how unity principles operate in the real world
(C) give an example that can serve as a point of comparison
(D) explain how an issue important to many people with power can significantly unify a country
(E) show how American political liberties can give rise to disunity in fringe groups

The subject matter of this passage is fairly common for the LSAT. Here, the author showcases the findings of an academic that relate to a way of understanding society. The author also elaborates on those findings.

1. *Main point*

The first question for this passage is also common. Here it is again:

1. The passage's main point can best be expressed as:

(A) No other country in the history of the world has been as unified as the United States.
(B) A nation's level of unity can be understood by studying a number of factors.
(C) Economic power is best achieved with a high level of unity.
(D) The world's problems can be solved more effectively through a unified approach.
(E) A large number of power points can nonetheless be tightly unified.

Answer choice B is the correct response because it encapsulates the whole discussion on "power points" and the related discussion on power in the first paragraph.

Answer choice A is incorrect because the passage analyzes the structure of unity in societies in general, not just that of the United States. Answer choice C is tempting because the passage does discuss economic power and its relationship to unity at some length. However, the passage goes beyond analyzing just that relationship, and thus this answer choice is too narrow.

Answer choice D is plainly wrong because the passage does not discuss how to solve world problems. Answer choice E is a valid conclusion about what the passage says about unity in the United States. It is not however, a valid statement about what the entire passage says.

2. *Inference about two items mentioned in the passage*

Question number two is also common. It basically asks you to make an inference. Here it is again:

2. According to the information presented in the passage about the interplay between unity and power:

(A) The most powerful power point will always prevail against other power points.
(B) Beliefs are usually not as powerful as people in a society.
(C) Chinese society handled internal tension in a manner that increased its power.
(D) The United States will most likely continue to increase its power because it remains unified.
(E) If not properly managed, conflict in Israel could tear the country apart.

Answer choice A is too extreme and is not entirely consistent with the passage. The example of a collision of power points in China shows how conflicting power points can work together, rather than one prevailing over the other. Answer choice B cannot be concluded from the passage. In fact, powerful beliefs are discussed in the passage, such as the belief in God and in Communism.

Answer choice C is correct. This answer choice articulates the outcome of the interplay between free market reforms and communism in China. Answer choice D is tempting because the reader could come to this conclusion based on the information in the passage. However, the passage does not say anything directly about the future of the United States. Thus, answer choice C is better.

Likewise, answer choice E can be validly concluded from the passage. However, the passage simply lists Israel as an example of distant power points, and does not directly say what the consequence of such distance is.

3. *Author's belief*
Here is question number 3 again:

3. Based on the information in the passage, Professor Gordon believes:

(A) Politicians would be able to better govern their countries if they understood unity and how to favorably influence the factors that go into the analysis of how unified a society is.
(B) Wars could be avoided if neighboring countries understood the makeup of power in each other and worked toward a constructive resolution to issues that divide them.
(C) Conflict is less likely if power in a society is highly dispersed among a group of people that are towards the middle of the political spectrum of a country.
(D) There has not been a power point as strong as the belief in economic prosperity in the United States among most citizens.
(E) It is possible to assemble different kinds of data into a numerical value that can provide a meaningful comparison of a level of unity that exists in societies at a given point in time.

Answer choice E is correct because it describes what Professor Gordon is doing. While the other answer choices could be correct, none of them follow from the passage. Answer choice A is wrong because there is no indication of how the information Professor Gordon has gathered should be used. That is why answer choice B is also incorrect.

Answer choices C and D are both wrong for the same reason. They both take statements about what exists in the United States and seek to apply it more broadly. The passage does not indicate that Professor Gordon believes in such an analysis.

4. *Inference relating to the theme*

Question four asks you to arrive at a conclusion about unity that is consistent with the analysis in the passage. Here is the question:

4. According to the information provided in the passage, a country is probably most unified if:

(A) it can exercise its power on other countries effectively
(B) most of its people adhere to most of the same beliefs
(C) many of its people share significant priorities
(D) it does not have a wide political spectrum with vastly different views
(E) most of its citizens have the spirit of cooperation to overcome differences

Answer choice A is wrong because the passage discusses how a country can be unified internally, and does not discuss influences of other countries. Answer choice B is wrong because it is not the best answer. In the United States, a unified country, the author indicates that there is debate about a variety of issues, including welfare, highways, and other matters.

Answer choice C is correct because it articulates the strong unity of the United States. While its people disagree on a number of issues, there is wide agreement on the pursuit of economic prosperity. Answer choice D is wrong because the United States is highly unified and has a wide political spectrum. Answer choice E is wrong because the passage does not discuss how to overcome differences.

5. *Inference about a concept discussed throughout the passage*

Here is question five:

5. The passage most supports which of the following statements about "power points" in a society?

(A) They are a significant factor that affects the analysis of how unified a country is.
(B) Significant power points are different in every country.
(C) They are largely beyond the control of any single person.
(D) Most people are unaware of how influential these points are.
(E) They are often destructive because they usually compete with each other.

Answer choice A is correct. The author calls power points "Another factor affecting unity" in the second paragraph of the passage. From the rest of the information in the passage one can conclude that this is a significant factor.

Answer choice B is wrong because the passage does not make statements about "every country". Answer choice C is wrong because it is not at all supported in the passage. If anything, things like communism and a belief in prosperity are widely recognized by people.

Answer choice E is wrong because it does not reflect what the passage says. The passage does say that when power points *collide* there is often destruction. But, the passage does not speak of the effect that power points usually have on each other.

6. *Main purpose of part of the passage*
Here is question six:

6. The function of the second to the last paragraph is most likely to:

(A) establish how the United States is superior to other countries in its form of social organization
(B) show how unity principles operate in the real world
(C) give an example that can serve as a point of comparison
(D) explain how an issue important to many people with power can significantly unify a country
(E) show how American political liberties can give rise to disunity in fringe groups

Answer choice D is correct. The passage indicates that many people in the United States have power, and that prosperity is a significant issue for those people. Answer choice A is wrong because the paragraph does not specifically compare the United States with other countries. Answer choice B is wrong because the passage does not discuss principles. The passage is an analysis of the nature of unity. Answer choice C is wrong because, as was mentioned above, this paragraph does not specifically compare the United States to other countries. Answer choice E is wrong because the passage does not speak of disunity in the fringe groups, nor does it mention the reason for why those groups exist.

D. Exam Techniques Applied To The Reading Passage
On the next page is a reproduction of the reading passage discussed above. The reproduced passage has markings that reflect the exam techniques discussed in this section. The crossed out portions of the question stems are written here to help you focus on what's important. They are not markings you should make when practicing for, or taking, the exam.

The unity of the United States is what has made it so powerful over its history. Professor Gordon has studied this phenomenon and has developed a "unity quotient". To arrive at this quotient Professor Gordon studied a number of factors that relate to political unity in a country. One important factor is the location of power in a society. Certain societies have a lot of power concentrated in the hands of a few people. In others, power is dispersed throughout the population.

Another factor affecting unity is the number of what Professor Gordon calls "power points" in a society. Those points can be either a person who is a leader, or an ideology that people follow. Power points can collide in a society, and sometimes that is beneficial. For example, in China in the 1980s Deng Xiaopeng was a person who represented a major power point in that country. He advocated free market reforms that were contrary to the communist ideology of China. The result of this collision of power points was economic growth within a framework of political stability. More often, the results of those collisions are civil wars.

A third unity factor is the distance between power points. The further the distance between power points, the less unity exists in a country. Israel is a country with perhaps the biggest distance between power points. Some of its residents, which include radical elements of its Arab population, advocate the destruction of the country. Orthodox Jews on the other hand, view the country as an institution established by God.

The United States has almost an ideal alignment of unity factors. While there is a large political spectrum in the United States, few citizens share the views that represent the ends of the spectrum. For example, the Communist Party exists in the United States, but does not have many members. The vast majority of political power is spread throughout a huge midsection of American voters. By far the biggest issue for those voters is economic prosperity. That is perhaps the biggest power point in American society, and there is not a lot of debate about how to achieve such prosperity. Almost all debate centers on how to spend the less than 10 percent of the budget that relates to welfare, highways, and other miscellaneous matters.

Real tension, leading to disunity, has arisen only once in the history of the United States. The Civil War occurred because power groups in different regions of the country had a fundamentally different approach to achieving the ideal of economic prosperity. For the South, such prosperity would be achieved through the free labor of slaves. For the North, prosperity would be achieved through innovative industries that would hire workers in the labor market. After the War, many African Americans seized hold of that ideal by moving to the north to work in factories. Southern industries have also seized hold of innovation, making the region one of the most vibrant areas of the country.

1. The passage's main point can best be expressed as:

(A) No other country in the history of the world has been as unified as the United States.
(B) A nation's level of unity can be understood by studying a number of factors.
(C) Economic power is best achieved with a high level of unity.
(D) The world's problems can be solved more effectively through a unified approach.
(E) A large number of power points can nonetheless be tightly unified.

2. According to the information presented in the passage about the interplay between unity and power:

(A) The most powerful power point will always prevail against other power points.
(B) Beliefs are usually not as powerful as people in a society.
(C) Chinese society handled internal tension in a manner that increased its power.
(D) The United States will most likely continue to increase its power because it remains unified.
(E) If not properly managed, conflict in Israel could tear the country apart.

GO ON TO THE NEXT PAGE.

3. Based on the information in the passage, Professor Gordon believes:

(A) Politicians would be able to better govern their countries if they understood unity and how to favorably influence the factors that go into the analysis of how unified a society is.

(B) Wars could be avoided if neighboring countries understood the makeup of power in each other and worked toward a constructive resolution to issues that divide them.

(C) Conflict is less likely if power in a society is highly dispersed among a group of people that are towards the middle of the political spectrum of a country.

(D) There has not been a power point as strong as the belief in economic prosperity in the United States among most citizens.

(E) It is possible to assemble different kinds of data into a numerical value that can provide a meaningful comparison of a level of unity that exists in societies at a given point in time.

4. According to the information provided in the passage, a country is probably most unified if:

(A) it can exercise its power on other countries effectively

(B) most of its people adhere to most of the same beliefs

(C) many of its people share significant priorities

(D) it does not have a wide political spectrum with vastly different views

(E) most of its citizens have the spirit of cooperation to overcome differences

5. The passage most supports which of the following statements about "power points" in a society?

(A) They are a significant factor that affects the analysis of how unified a country is.

(B) Significant power points are different in every country.

(C) They are largely beyond the control of any single person.

(D) Most people are unaware of how influential these points are.

(E) They are often destructive because they usually compete with each other.

6. The function of the second to the last paragraph is most likely to:

(A) establish how the United States is superior to other countries in its form of social organization

(B) show how unity principles operate in the real world

(C) give an example that can serve as a point of comparison

(D) explain how an issue important to many people with power can significantly unify a country

(E) show how American political liberties can give rise to disunity in fringe groups

Now, it is a good idea to review the "Tools for Taking the Entire Exam" in section II of this book. Subsection A, entitled "Time Is Money, and LSAT Time Is Expensive," is particularly important.

VI. WRITING SAMPLE
The writing sample part of the exam should be a low priority in your preparation because it is difficult to gauge how much it will help you. Law schools pay close attention to U.S. News & World Report rankings of law schools because they want to appear high in those rankings. While law schools for the most part do not endorse the rankings, the reality is that the rankings have a huge impact on applicants' decisions on where to go to law school. The best applicants choose to attend the best ranked schools.

A law school will not boost its ranking position by taking into account the writing sample portion of the LSAT. U.S. News & World Report does not look (and probably cannot look) at writing samples when preparing its rankings. Because law schools want to show they admit students who scored highly on the LSAT, they will probably admit those kinds of students even if their writing sample was unimpressive. That being said, you do not want to look bad on the writing sample.

Avoid studying for the writing sample until you know which administration of the exam you will take. The Law School Admissions Council, which produces the LSAT, has been experimenting with changing the writing sample format. The Council advises that examples of the kinds of writing sample questions that will appear on each administration of the exam will be found on its website at www.lsac.org. Thus, when you decide which administration of the exam you will take, check that website to find out what to expect in terms of a writing sample question.

In the past, these questions have presented test takers with two options. Test takers were asked to write an essay supporting one of the options and critiquing the other. For example, the question would indicate that someone has the choice of purchasing one of two products. You are then told one of the products must be selected on the basis of two criteria, like price and quality. Finally, you are given two paragraphs, each with information concerning the two choices.

One way to write an essay in response to this kind of question is to divide it into two parts. In the first, you explain why your position should prevail. In the second, explain why the contrary position should be opposed. Each of these two sections can be subdivided into the two criteria that the question gives you. Explain how, in light of the facts, each of the criteria support your position and oppose the contrary position.

VII. PHYSICAL PREPARATIONS

There are a number of things you should do to physically prepare for the exam.

A. Exercise regularly in the months before the exam
If you do not already have a regular exercise routine, get into one in the months before the exam. It will help alleviate stress and increase your mental strength. A simple, effective, and accessible form of exercise is to go on a brisk walk for one hour every day. Start slow and gradually increase intensity over the span of several days.

B. Control your diet

In the months before the exam, minimize stress by cutting down on salty foods. If you are not a regular coffee drinker, get into the habit of drinking coffee in the mornings, because it has been proven to increase your concentration.

For breakfast on the day of the exam have pancakes with plenty of syrup and a cup of coffee. The syrup will give you instant energy and the pancakes will give you other kinds of energy to carry you through the morning. The coffee will also give you energy and increase your concentration.

Avoid eating cold cereal and drinking lots of coffee because you do not want to use the restroom during the exam.

C. Scope Out The Test Center

Find out where the exam will be administered and drive there on the day of the week and at the time that the exam will be administered, which will usually be a Saturday. Pay close attention to how long it takes you to get there. Find a parking place close to the test center and walk around the center's neighborhood. Become familiar with the roads in the area and any other parking places, should they become necessary on the day of the exam. If there is an accident that causes a traffic jam on the day of the exam, you want to have a strategy for getting to the exam on time nonetheless.

Walk around the test center. See where the restrooms and drinking fountain are.

Walk around inside the test room and find its air vents. Sit in a chair, place your time piece and some pencils on the table to get a feel for exactly what it will be like on the day of the exam. If possible, take a practice exam in that room.

D. Do not significantly alter your schedule during the weeks before the exam

The best way to take the mystery, and stress, out of the testing experience is to take practice exams in the month before the exam on the same day of the week and during the same time of the day that the actual exam will be administered. This way you know you will not be surprised and you will be thoroughly familiar with the test experience.

Cramming for the exam in the days before can create stress and uncertainty because you will be unsure of how your recently acquired knowledge will play out in a regular testing environment.

E. On the night before the exam, relax

You will have more strength on the day of the exam if you sleep well the night before. However, if you are not able to get a complete night's sleep, don't worry. Most other test takers probably also will not have had a good night's sleep either.

F. Bring appropriate gear

On the day of the exam you should have the following equipment:

1. Layered clothing
This will help you comfortably adjust to the room's temperature

2. Silent timepiece

A stop watch is the best time tool because you can trigger it at the beginning of each section. If you don't have one (or do not want to buy one) take a watch. When the proctor says "begin," note on your test booklet how many minutes the watch is different from the start time. For example, if the test starts when your watch says "9:06 AM," then place a +6 sign on the booklet to remind you that you need to adjust the time on the clock by six minutes to let you know exactly how much time you have during the exam. If this is too cumbersome for you, investing in a stop watch is probably the best way to go.

3. Energy booster

Place a snack that gives you energy in one of your pockets. During a break in the exam, eat or drink it quickly. The boost will help your concentration and energy level during the last part of the exam.

4. Everything the test takers tell you to bring

Be sure to bring a form of ID and anything else the test takers tell you to bring.

VIII. OTHER TIP: PLAN TO TAKE THE EXAM ONLY ONCE

Don't plan on taking the exam more than once. If do you take the exam over, your first score will go on your record and it can become a factor that law schools look at (how much of a factor varies from school to school). You will probably gain very little additional knowledge of the exam by actually taking it. Later on, the exam you take will simply become one more prior exam that you will have access to. So, when you take the exam, do so with the intention of taking it just once.

If, for whatever reason, you think you should take the exam over, consider canceling your score rather than letting your score register. Based on your performance on practice exams, you should have a good idea of how well you did on the actual exam. Waiting to get your score in the hopes that you got lucky and scored better than you did in practice exams is an option, but probably not a good idea for something as important as the LSAT.

IX. CONCLUDING THOUGHTS

The LSAT may lead you to a new appreciation for the subtleties and complexities of the English language. I think of the exam as "English on steroids" or "neon English" (as opposed to the less intense English we use in everyday life). Regardless, this book will almost certainly have boosted your score. A higher score will boost your chances of getting into a better school. That in turn will give you more influence over how our world works.

I hope you use that influence to make the world a better place.

Appendix A

Crash Course

If you bought this book one week before the exam and just want a few tips so that you won't have to retake the exam, here's the plan for you:

1. Read this book so that you understand the exam and the strategies for attacking it.
2. Practice war games, because that is where your performance will probably improve the most.
3. Take the practice exam attached to this book without timing yourself, grade it, and understand why you got each question right or wrong. Then re-read the parts of this book that address the areas where you need to improve.
4. Finally, bring a good luck charm with you on the day of the exam!

Appendix B

Standard Approach

Structure your study time if you plan to allocate a significant amount of time to study for this important exam. Create a flexible plan that you can change as you discover how you improve. Don't allocate specific amounts of time to studying for specific sections of the exam.

Take the opportunities for improvement wherever you see them.

Here's a checklist of what you should do:

1. Read this book;
2. Budget a certain amount of study time (many people budget two months);
3. Take the practice exam in this book. Don't time yourself, and read the explanations for why you got answers right or wrong.
4. Purchase twenty previously administered LSATs. Don't take the oldest one or the four most recent ones (I'll explain later), but take the next four exams, and time yourself (Thus, you would take exams 2 through 16 of the 20 exams you purchase.).
5. Plot all your grades for each section of each exam on graphs and examine how (or if) you have improved.
6. If your grades in all three sections maintain a generally upward direction, continue taking practice exams, beginning with the older ones.
7. When your grades on one section reach a plateau, follow the guidelines on dealing with plateaus that are outlined below.
8. After you have reviewed why you have reached a plateau, and after developing a response to address those reasons, put that response into practice by taking another five practice exams.
9. After you have reviewed why you have reached a plateau in all three subject areas of the exam, developed a response to address the reasons why, and have put that response into practice, your job is almost over.
10. Using the four most recently administered exams, take one practice exam per week on each of the four weekends before the actual exam. Save the oldest, previously administered exam and insert one section of that exam into each of these four exams. The sections of the oldest exam will function as the ungraded section found on the actual LSAT. Making that section part of your practice exams will give you a feel for what taking the entire exam is like. It will help you develop your stamina for the entire length of the exam.

Appendix C

Exhaustive Approach

This approach is for the person who wants to spend the time and resources to fully develop his or her potential for taking the LSAT. People who take this approach usually want to get into the best law school possible. If you have enough natural exam-taking ability, this approach can lead you to the perfect 180 score.

Here's a checklist:

1. Carefully read this book.
2. Be single-mindedly goal oriented.

    Plan to take the exam after you have spent however much time it will take you to reach your *full* potential on the exam. The length of study will vary depending on each person's natural exam-taking ability. You should keep comprehensive report cards to track your progress (see section II.D "Generate a Rigorous Report Card" on how to do this) so that you can clearly establish when you reach your full potential.

    Don't set a time limit for your studies. How do you realistically do this? The best way to allocate what could become a significant amount of study time is to combine your LSAT studies with your college studies, an internship, or your job. Make studying a routine part of your life. Think of it as a regular mental exercise regime that you perform just like other forms of exercising, like jogging or swimming.

    You can make exam practice a regular part of your life by doing questions whenever you get pockets of free time. Logic questions are best suited for this because they are short. You can do a few while waiting for a bus. Reading comprehension and war game questions require larger blocks of time, which you may have if you commute by sitting in a train or bus. Practicing in those environments, with some distractions, may benefit you because on the day of the exam you will not be in an environment with complete peace and quiet. You could have a neighbor who makes an annoying noise with his pencil, or who has a cough and sneezes regularly, or the vent system in the room may rattle and blow cool air directly on you.

    On weekends take more time to do larger sets of reading comprehension or war game questions, or entire practice exams. If you have a job that simply does not allow you to take much time off, or if your job is mentally exhausting so that you do not have the energy to focus your studies, consider changing jobs, or, consider taking time off.
3. Take the practice exam in this book, don't time yourself, and read the explanations for why you got questions right and wrong.
4. Keep a journal of the issues you face and the things you learn.
5. Purchase other study aids with practice exams, take four exams, and time yourself.

    Other study aids with practice exams are generally not quite as useful as previously administered exams, but they are good places to start practicing. I think exams by The Princeton Review are the best, but other books, available through places like Barnes &

Noble and Borders, will do the job. You should start out with them and develop your understanding of the exam through practice, practice, practice.

If your grades in all three sections maintain a generally upward direction, continue to take entire practice exams.

6. Purchase previously administered exams

7. When your grades on one section of the exam reach a plateau, move on to take previously administered LSAT exams, beginning with the older ones. Do not take the oldest exam or the four most recently administered exams (you'll see why below). If you obtain similar scores to those you obtained on practice exams in study aids, follow the guidelines on dealing with plateaued grades in section II.F of this book entitled "What if my scores plateau?"

8. If you study for about ten months, take a one month vacation from studying. After your vacation, once again review the general guidelines for taking the exam in this book.

9. Everyday, for one week, take sets of about 25 questions in the areas of the exam where you think you can make the most improvement. To review, take one set of about 25 questions in the areas where you think you have reached your full potential.

10. Take five practice exams and examine whether your scores follow the same plateau pattern they have before.

11. Examine the kinds of questions you got wrong and make a judgment about whether you will be able to get those questions right by taking additional practice exams. If you cannot get those kinds of questions consistently right, then CONGRATULATIONS! You have reached your full potential on the exam!

12. If you think you can, with more practice, improve your performance, do more practice exams and once again reevaluate your performance.

13. Take each of the four most recently administered exams on each of the four weekends before the actual exam. Take the oldest previously administered exam and insert one section of that exam into each of these four exams. The sections of the oldest exam function as the ungraded section found on the actual LSAT. Making that section part of your practice exams will give you a feel for what taking the entire exam is like. It will help you develop stamina for the entire length of the exam.

Appendix D

Practice Exam

The following exam does not have directions and other markings that are on the actual exam. You should not pay attention to the markings that are not included in this exam because they will probably not help you increase your score.

35 minutes

1.   The Slenderhead fish in Spear Lake need oxygenated water to breathe and live healthy lives. The state electric authority recently granted Power Co. a permit to build a power plant close to the lake and use lake water to cool its turbines. Warm water from the plant will make algae grow and that algae will consume oxygen in the water, causing the level of oxygen in the lake to decline. The State has acted irresponsibly by endangering the future of the Slenderhead in Spear Lake.

The above conclusion depends on which of the following assumptions:

  (A) The power plant will cause the level of oxygen in the lake water to decline to levels at which Slenderhead fish may not be able to survive.
  (B) The State can act responsibly only if it denies Power Co. a permit to build a plant close to the lake.
  (C) Slenderhead fish are not an endangered species because they live in many other lakes.
  (D) Slenderhead fish are an endangered species that can only reproduce in Spear Lake.
  (E) Only the State, and not the Federal government, is responsible for the wellbeing of wildlife.

2.   The effort expended by a human being running five miles per hour creates a noticeable level of fatigue in the muscles of the heart. Because specialized medical devices exist that can detect that fatigue, we will be able to screen out astronaut candidates that pose a risk of heart failure.

Which of the following most seriously weakens the argument?

  (A) Most people are unaware of any level of fatigue in their heart when they run at that speed.
  (B) The level of fatigue in heart muscles does not affect the risk of heart failure.
  (C) Other factors, such as intelligence, are more important in an astronaut.
  (D) In the past astronauts have not been screened with this technology.
  (E) Fatigue is only one factor that affects a person's likelihood of heart failure.

3.   Expert: Conflict is often thought of as being destructive because it can impede cooperation among the conflicting parties. However, the benefits of conflict should not be overlooked because they have been substantial. Wars have not only served as catalysts for innovation, they have forged a unity that has led to a prosperity in nations that would not exist otherwise.

The main point of the above reasoning can best be expressed as:

  (A) Conflict is more beneficial than it is destructive.
  (B) Without conflict people become unproductively complacent.
  (C) If there were more conflict, there would be more prosperity.
  (D) Cooperation mixed with conflict is the optimum solution.
  (E) Conflict has been beneficial amidst destructive events.

4.   Declaring bankruptcy is painful. It hinders a person's ability to obtain credit for many years and landlords may refuse to rent property. Personal debt burdens are harmful only if the debts cannot be paid for many years. Often, people find that if they work harder and live a simpler lifestyle they can make payments on their debts. Therefore, people should not declare bankruptcy unless there is simply no way they will be able to repay their debts.

Which of the following principles, if true, supports the above reasoning?

  (A) A process that is definitely painful should not be used to address a situation that can potentially be resolved.
  (B) Pain should be avoided with hard work.
  (C) It is better to be a good person than to live irresponsibly and depend on painful solutions.
  (D) Harmful circumstances can always be avoided with careful planning.
  (E) Long term solutions work best to address short term problems

GO OVER TO THE NEXT PAGE.

5. Chuck: Few people from the Ton Ton tribe have served on the council, despite the fact that many people from other tribes are on the council. Therefore, either Ton Ton tribe members are not as politically active as other tribes, or the council has unfairly excluded them.

Mary: The Ton Ton tribe is small compared to other tribes that are several times its size. Thus, it is possible that there are proportionally more Ton Ton members on the council than there are members of other tribes.

Which of the following most closely describes Mary's response?

(A) She establishes that the groups Chuck compares do not have significant commonalities.
(B) She uses competing data to question Chuck's conclusion.
(C) She uses information that undermines the accuracy of Chuck's information.
(D) She calls into question Chuck's conclusion by establishing that he uses absolute numbers instead of proportions.
(E) She demonstrates Chuck has improperly defined the groups he compares.

6. The use of diets as the primary method of strengthening the body is a misguided approach to fitness. The focus should be on exercise. The body is able to convert foods of average nutritional value into the many kinds of nutrients it needs. However, the body does not generate muscle in the absence of exercise. Exercise is therefore critical and should be the main focus of a wellness routine.

Which of the following most strengthens the above argument?

(A) Most diets do not work because people who are on them don't make an effort to exercise.
(B) Through exercise the body not only increases muscle tissue, but also increases its ability to convert food into needed nutrients.
(C) The dieting industry is so filled with questionable "easy, no pain" solutions that it is best not to even try to find a useful diet.
(D) Exercise makes you more hungry, making it less necessary to diet.
(E) Celebrities who succeeded the most have strong bodies, but do not promote diets.

7. Student: A university education is something that certain successful people have, but not all successful people have a university education. Furthermore, there are people who attended a university, and who even obtained good grades, who are not successful. Thus, a university education does not create successful people.

The student's reasoning is most clearly called into question by the fact that it:

(A) provides a questionable justification for not being industrious.
(B) is narrow in its focus on "success" in life, when there are many other things worth striving for.
(C) concludes that a link between education and success does not exist because it does not always exist.
(D) ignores the fact that unsuccessful university graduates may be unsuccessful for reasons not related to their education.
(E) is limited in its analysis of university graduates when there is a huge variety of education levels.

8. Modern art represents a substantial increase in the creative bandwidth available to artists. Unlike past art forms, such as Impressionism and artistic styles used during the Renaissance, modern art is not bound by the forms, shapes or colors that are found in scenes observed in nature. Modern art has the potential to fully unleash the creative energy of artistic minds.

The argument's main conclusion is best stated as being:

(A) Modern art allows for a greater variety of expression than prior art forms.
(B) Freedom of expression is the most important factor for identifying good art.
(C) Modern art is better, even if it is harder to understand than other forms of art.
(D) Good art is a matter of taste in the eye of the beholder, not in the freedom of the artist.
(E) Prior art forms would have been better if they allowed for more freedom of expression.

GO OVER TO THE NEXT PAGE.

9. Eating spicy chicken can cause stomach cramps in people that are not used to eating spicy food. While Bob was on a long trip he got stomach cramps and was not able to relax. Bob must have eaten spicy chicken, or at least some spicy food.

The conclusion is vulnerable to the criticism that:

(A) It changes its use of "cramps" from "discomfort" to "inability to relax."
(B) It considers one event that can cause a second event as being necessary for the occurrence of the second event.
(C) It uses irrelevant information to support its reasoning.
(D) It uses an overbroad rule to arrive at the conclusion.
(E) It ignores the possibility that Bob was eating unfamiliar food.

10. Books printed with new technology have an average of only 2 defects for every 10 books printed. With two quality inspections a printing company can deliver a thousand books with a total of only 15 defects. Therefore, it is cost effective to do just two quality inspections for most books.

This reasoning is most susceptible to critique on which of the following grounds?

(A) It fails to consider the fact that it is possible that all defects would be detected with one additional inspection.
(B) The cost of defects can be huge because customers for some books become extremely upset when they see even one defect.
(C) The author arrives at the conclusion without weighing the costs and benefits of additional improvements.
(D) Some books are really expensive to print, so it is better to print them right rather than to do a quality check later.
(E) Investment in even better printing technology will improve books more than spending more on quality control.

11. Squeaks and rattling can be heard in some cars that have been on rough roads, or that have run over a sudden bump at a high speed on the freeway. Those noises can be indications that the car will become unsafe, such as if a piece of the drivetrain is loose, or if the braking system is becoming undone. However, all cars develop noises as they age, and such noises are not always indications of danger. The same is true of cars that have been on rough roads.

The conclusion of the above statements can best be expressed as:

(A) Newer cars are safer than cars that have squeaks and rattling.
(B) In general, cars that have been on rough roads are less safe than other cars.
(C) People should pay attention to the maintenance needs of their car so that noises do not develop.
(D) Squeaks and rattling in a car that has been on rough roads are not necessarily indications of danger.
(E) Rough roads should be avoided because they are harder on your car than other roads.

12. Student: The island of Tikilaka is a good place to take a vacation because all my friends who have been there loved it. All major cruise lines regularly dock in its harbor and every major airline has flights to its busy airport.

The above reasoning assumes that:

(A) The friends who have gone to Tikilaka can accurately assess whether the island is a good vacation destination.
(B) Tikilaka's busy harbor and airport do not distract from the fact that the island is a good place to take a vacation.
(C) The friends who have gone to Tikilaka were there on vacation.
(D) The views of the friends who have been to Tikilaka are representative of people who have visited that island.
(E) Tikilaka's airport and harbor are busy because of the tourism industry.

GO OVER TO THE NEXT PAGE.

13. Activist: Immigrants from African countries to the United States have, relative to the general American population, a disproportionately low level of advanced degrees. This is further evidence of racial discrimination by the white majority establishment against black African immigrants.

If true, which of the following most seriously calls into question the above conclusion?

(A) African immigrants have less education when they immigrate than the general American population.
(B) African immigrants have a higher proportion of advanced degrees than the people in their countries of origin.
(C) White immigrants from Eastern Europe also have a disproportionately low level of advanced degrees.
(D) Asian immigrants pursue advanced degrees more vigorously than do immigrants from other regions.
(E) The American population maintains its vitality with the influx of ambitious immigrants seeking a better future.

14. Researcher: A recent study concluded that most cancers cannot be prevented by good eating habits. The study found that people who eat a healthy diet die of cancer at a higher rate than other people. However, people who eat a healthy diet live longer than other people, and the incidence of cancer rises in older people regardless of what diet they follow.

The researcher's main point can best be described as:

(A) People should be encouraged to eat a healthy diet because a balanced intake of nutrients is good for you.
(B) The study's conclusion about healthy eating is called into question by the incidence of cancer in elderly people.
(C) The study is flawed because healthy eating is obviously good for you, even if it may have some bad side effects.
(D) If you want to live a long life, you should eat a healthy diet and prepare yourself for the ailments that will afflict you later in life.
(E) A healthy diet does not have any adverse consequences, and the study's conclusion to the contrary is the result of incomplete analysis.

15. Teacher: To be a good leader you first have to know how to be a good follower. Many leaders ignore this concept and, in doing so, are ineffective because they do not appreciate how their actions will resonate with their followers. Only good leaders have good followers, because it is not possible to be a good follower of a bad leader.

Which of these must also be true if the Teacher's conclusions are correct?

(A) Good leaders are hard to come by because most people would rather follow someone else, even if that person is a bad leader.
(B) Leadership, whether good or bad, is acquired only through experience and is not the product of natural ability.
(C) To overcome the shortcomings of your leaders you must seek to be more effective by being sensitive to how your actions resonate with others.
(D) If someone is a good leader, then at some point they were a follower of another good leader from whom they learned good leadership.
(E) People who believe they are good leaders should first consider whether their leaders were effective.

16. Though the reason for why they cure people has never been fully understood, herbal extracts have been a part of alternative medicine treatments for millennia. But, with advances in herbal extract testing techniques and the decoding of ancient medical texts that describe how certain extracts were discovered, modern medicine will now be able to understand and cooperate closely with people who practice alternative medicine.

The above argument depends on the following assumption:

(A) Understanding and cooperation are possible, even if discoveries about the extracts challenge modern medicine's views of alternative medicine.
(B) Modern medicine cannot cooperate closely with alternative medicine if it does not understand how herbal extracts work.
(C) Herbal extracts are a significant part of alternative medicinal treatments.
(D) The reasons herbal extracts cure people will be discovered and accepted by modern medicine.
(E) Herbal extracts do in fact cure people.

GO OVER TO THE NEXT PAGE.

17. Chacho: Young parents in a survey indicated that they do not usually sleep well because their children wake them up constantly. Couples without children reported that they are generally healthy and relaxed. Having children does not enhance the well-being of parents because parents with children reported lower levels of wellness than other couples.
Lani: But children often take care of their parents when they are unable to care for themselves.

Of the following, which best describes Lani's response to Chacho's argument?

(A) She indicates that Chacho is correct, but for a different reason.
(B) It establishes a flaw in the survey's methodology.
(C) It offers information that calls into question Chacho's conclusion.
(D) Lani indicates Chacho assumes his conclusion is true.
(E) Lani argues Chacho's conclusion is incorrect because he did not consider important information.

18. Economist: The substantial drop in labor costs during the last quarter was highly beneficial for the economy because it helped make goods cheaper for everybody. If goods were not cheaper, the economy would not have expanded, and the country would instead have gone into a deep recession. Therefore, the drop in labor costs kept the country out of recession.

The economist's argument can be called into question because:

(A) it does not consider the possibility that lower labor costs mean lower wages for poor working people
(B) it does not consider the possibility that goods may have gotten cheaper even without lower labor costs
(C) it does not take into account the many factors that go into the analysis of a country's economy
(D) economists, unlike investors, only analyze data about the past and do not seek to predict the future
(E) cheaper goods are only one of many different ways that an economy can be stimulated, and kept out of a recession

19. As the computer revolution has progressed the amount of space and money required for computing power has decreased dramatically. In the earlier stages of the computer industry, this increase in efficiency allowed consumers to own a computer for entertainment purposes. In the industry's later stages, the more complex tasks required by small businesses could be accomplished by a computer purchased by a consumer.

Which of the following best articulates the information about the computer industry presented above?

(A) The increases in computing efficiency have empowered consumers to do more with computers they purchase.
(B) In the future big businesses will operate on computers used by consumers.
(C) The positive influence of the decline in the price for computing power is only now being fully realized.
(D) It is unlikely that in the future the computer revolution will be able to progress as much as it has in the past.
(E) It is a good idea for most consumers to take advantage of the many things they can now do with computers.

GO OVER TO THE NEXT PAGE.

20. In today's business environment trade secrets are more important than they have ever been in the past. The beverage industry, where the precise mixture of ingredients for a beverage can be a company's biggest asset, is a prime example of that reality. Only if the exact original recipe is followed can a beverage with the same fizz, sweetness and freshness be made.

If the above is true, which of these CANNOT be correct?

(A) Many additional beverages remain to be discovered, and that is why the existing trade secrets do not impede consumer choice.
(B) Companies maintain extensive procedures and controls to protect their recipes from competitors.
(C) Some beverage combinations, which have become widely used and highly profitable, were discovered by accident.
(D) With modern technology chemists are able to study beverages and come to conclusions about their makeup.
(E) Someone has, through research, made an exact reproduction of another company's secret beverage.

21. While gambling can be destructively addictive, it also has healthy entertainment value and can boost the economy of the area in and around a city with a gambling industry. To boost the economy and wellness of its citizens, the national legislature should promote gambling that has healthy entertainment value.

The above argument depends on the assumption that:

(A) It is possible to promote gambling in a manner that, on balance, improves the life of citizens.
(B) The entertainment value of gambling outweighs its destructive addictiveness.
(C) The improved economic conditions in gambling cities do not come at the expense of other communities.
(D) On a national scale, people want to gamble.
(E) The life of citizens can be improved through promoting gambling more so than through promoting anything else.

22. Commercial: Buy Timber Trucks because they are better than other trucks. A recent study found Timber Trucks are cheaper and used less gas on average than other trucks in their class. Farmer George has been using Timber Trucks for over 30 years and says "I would not trade my truck for anything."

All of the following establish a reason to question the commercial EXCEPT:

(A) The facts presented were not compiled by an independent source.
(B) An older Timber Truck could be hard to purchase.
(C) A general conclusion about Timber Trucks is arrived at based on limited criteria.
(D) The durability of the Timber Truck compared to other trucks is not established.
(E) No facts concerning the safety of the trucks are considered.

GO OVER TO THE NEXT PAGE.

79

23. Advertisement: Using doctor recommended Handlea cream regularly is the best way to make you appear younger because it makes wrinkles on your face disappear. Studies have repeatedly shown that people who use Handlea cream are perceived to be younger than their actual age.

For this to be an effective advertisement:

(A) The studies cited must be accurate, even though the people studied may not have used the cream regularly.
(B) There must be no better way to get rid of wrinkles.
(C) Readers with wrinkles must want to appear younger.
(D) Readers must trust what is said, even though it is an advertisement.
(E) Having a young appearance is a good thing.

24. The seashell deposits on Point Lalton, a popular tourist attraction, have fluctuated over the years. A storm can wash large quantities of seashells on to the point's beaches, where tourists pick out the brighter and more colorful shells. Sometimes currents around the point shift and erode accumulations of shells. Seashell deposits on Point Lalton are at an all time low, so a storm will surely sweep over the point soon.

The above reasoning assumes that:

(A) The level of seashell deposits on the point is related to the probability of a storm sweeping through the point.
(B) Storms do not assail the point when it has large seashell deposits.
(C) Low levels of seashell deposits cause storms on Point Lalton.
(D) Shifting currents that erode seashell deposits signal a change to a weather pattern that will cause a storm.
(E) Tourists have not removed a significant number of seashells from the point.

GO OVER TO THE NEXT PAGE.

25. To maintain a high level of speed during the entire Sparkling Diamond race, cars must stop to refuel at least three times. Racer Rob refueled only twice, but was first place in the race.

Which of the following explains the above outcome?

    (A) Racer Rob is an experienced driver with an advanced car.

    (B) An accident in the beginning of the race eliminated all contestants except for Racer Rob.

    (C) It is possible to finish the race faster by not operating at a high level of speed and avoiding one refuel stop.

    (D) Not all cars have the same level of fuel efficiency.

    (E) Technique, not just high levels of speed, can win a race.

26. A liberal arts education is more desirable than a technical degree for most of society's workers because, with it, students can apply core concepts to a wide variety of career paths. Courses leading to a technical degree often do not teach core concepts, and instead focus on specific sequences of tasks that will become obsolete as technology and the economy change.

If valid, which of these provides the strongest justification for the above reasoning?

    (A) Some of the most successful people in society have liberal arts degrees and report no interest in getting a technical degree.

    (B) Core concepts are more interesting, but more complex, than task sequences.

    (C) Workers' versatility because of their ability to apply core concepts substantially increases their well-being.

    (D) Jobs of a technical nature can be easily outsourced to other countries.

    (E) Liberal arts degree graduates have a higher IQ than technical degree graduates.

S T O P

35 minutes

The Mayas were a peace loving people until the Toltec influence appeared in their culture. The Mayas, though best known for their main pyramid at Chichen Itzá, were also avid sports enthusiasts. They played a game that is a precursor to modern basketball.

In this game, small hoops are attached high on the wall of a large courtyard. The players were allowed to use only their waist and ankles to touch the ball. Scoring was extremely difficult for that reason, and because the ball was only a little smaller than the hoops.

This sport provided a means for defusing tensions among subgroups of the Maya, the same way that modern sports do. However, that changed when the Toltecs arrived. This sport, rather than defusing tension, became an instrument for creating discord. The rules changed so that the captain of the losing team would get killed. This transformed the game into a battle of life and death, with an important person's life at stake. The deaths of such important people probably created resentment and hatred that would spill over into violence outside the game. This would be especially true if the outcome of the game was disputed. The effect of a bad call by the game's referee would be disastrous.

While the brutality of such a game is undeniable, it appears that participation in the game was voluntary. For religious reasons, or to acquire fame, players themselves enabled the violence. Thus, one can hardly feel sorry for the captains who lost their lives. They not only agreed to the process that killed them, but they made the process possible.

The victims of the violence that resulted from the sport however, were innocent. Their blood rests on the heads of the athletes and of the Toltecs.

It is difficult to arrive at definite conclusions about this game however, because we do not have a definite historical record about it. The Mayan civilization declined and the sport ceased to be played by the time the Spanish arrived. Shortly after their arrival, the Spanish destroyed almost all records pertaining to Mayan history.

What have survived, however, are the game courts. They have been reconstructed after the hoops alongside them had fallen off. The trees and shrubs that had overgrown the courts have been uprooted and grass once again grows in them. Some of the old game courts' acoustics are surprisingly good. At the court of Chichen Itzá, people can stand at the ends of the court, which is

at least 80 feet long, and talk to each other as if they were standing next to one another.

While the game was a source of death in its day, today it is a lifeblood for the local economy. Tourists spend several million dollars a year visiting the ruins and enjoying Mayan hospitality.

1. The author probably believes:

   (A) A lot of people died because of the game.
   (B) The Spanish were more violent than the Toltecs.
   (C) Mayan civilization declined because of the game.
   (D) Toltecs played the game better than the Mayas.
   (E) The game's new rules were not just.

2. Which of the following best describes the tone of the passage:

   (A) Indignation because of injustice.
   (B) Balanced historical analysis.
   (C) Confusion over a lack of information.
   (D) Impassioned advocacy for the rights of the oppressed.
   (E) Hopefulness for a better future.

GO OVER TO THE NEXT PAGE.

3. From this passage we can conclude:

    (A) Games are the most effective way to defuse social tension.
    (B) The Mayas were conquered by the Toltecs.
    (C) The game was entertaining.
    (D) The Mayas would have been better off discontinuing the game.
    (E) Most games were probably unfair because the stakes were so high.

4. The information about the Spanish is included to:

    (A) Qualify the statements made about the game's victims.
    (B) Place blame on the Spanish for the decline of the game.
    (C) Clarify why the Mayan civilization declined.
    (D) Explain why historical research is important.
    (E) Indicate a possible solution to the puzzle created by an incomplete historical record.

5. The passage is most consistent with which of the following statements:

    (A) Peoples of the past were more violent than those of the present.
    (B) Justice is served when there is a constructive mechanism for defusing social tension.
    (C) Games that involve death are always wrong.
    (D) We do not have enough information about the game to learn a lesson about it.
    (E) Modern sports at times can have the same problems that this game had.

GO OVER TO THE NEXT PAGE.

Income inequality is generally bad for a nation because it breeds violence, envy, and mistrust. Even if everyone in a society has enough wealth to live what most would consider a "normal comfortable life," people do not feel "normal" when they live in proximity to really wealthy people. Thus, they perceive themselves as being "poor" even though they may not be poor by an objective measure. This perception, though flawed, breeds violence, corruption and other social ills.

Having a society with complete equality has proven unworkable. Because people have different abilities, they inevitably acquire different levels of wealth over time. Thus, wealth would have to be periodically rebalanced even if it were spread equally at any point in time.

Also, there are some benefits to inequality. Certain good things, like substantial investments in new technology, require lots of money. While governments can, and often do, make such investments, they do not necessarily have the skills to do so for all potential new technological advances. A highly skilled wealthy person can sometimes accomplish complex things, like the invention of a new computer, that a government bureaucracy cannot do.

Thus, to maximize the total wealth created by humanity, a balance must be struck between having some inequality and not having any inequality. This is an extremely difficult task because it is almost impossible to identify which skilled people, if given wealth, would multiply the wealth. The most we can hope for is a somewhat random distribution of assets within a range of inequality. As crime rises and economic growth stalls, the government should implement wealth redistribution programs. Such redistribution will greatly benefit wealthy people. Aside from the obvious benefit of lower crime, there are other benefits. With more widely available resources, business and technological advances occur more often. Wealthy people benefit from those advances, such as better software, safer cars, and better medicines. Having less money is by itself beneficial for many wealthy people because wealth can create, rather than avoid, problems. With more wealth, there is more to manage, and also more things that can go wrong.

Most politicians focus on increases and decreases in inequality. A more constructive focus would be to study what the wealth gets spent on. That way, if wealthy people generate the most wealth with their wealth, then increasing inequality may be a good thing. Giving more money to the middle class so they can take more vacations and buy bigger televisions is not necessarily in society's best interest.

Too often, popular attitudes are shaped by images from extreme ends of the spectrum. People think of inequality in terms of the super rich in their yachts and mansions benefiting at the expense of poor people with no housing or food. Those attitudes are fed by sensationalism in the media, which focuses on dramatic subjects in the hope of attracting readership.

What is needed is careful analysis of how existing wealth is being used to generate additional wealth. Radical wealth redistribution based on sensationalist stories could actually decrease the overall level of wealth and the overall welfare of humanity.

6.   Based on the passage, which of the following best describes the author's attitude towards the poor:

(A) Irresponsible.
(B) Mistrustful.
(C) Sympathetic.
(D) Insensitive.
(E) Detached.

7.   The main point of the passage can best be articulated as being:

(A) Wellbeing and wealth are the same thing; therefore, social policy should seek to maximize both.
(B) Inequality should exist within a certain range because it is difficult to know how much inequality is beneficial.
(C) The media is irresponsible because it distorts the issues, thereby causing more inequality.
(D) It is not possible to have an appropriate policy regarding wealth because the subject matter is too complicated.
(E) Maximizing wealth, while difficult to do, can be accomplished if people are rewarded for their efforts.

GO OVER TO THE NEXT PAGE.

8. The author would most likely agree with a wealth redistribution plan that:

(A) Gives more money to the rich if they will not buy a yacht with it.
(B) Takes money from the poor if they do not spend it on things that are beneficial for them, such as food and housing.
(C) Creates a wealth allocation similar to an allocation that has created substantial wealth in the past.
(D) Does not give money to the middle class, because they usually do not spend their money in a manner that creates wealth.
(E) The author would not agree to any wealth redistribution plan.

9. The passage indicates that:

(A) Inequality is a good thing because complete equality is unworkable.
(B) Rebalancing wealth is too much work.
(C) Wealth redistribution can have non-monetary benefits.
(D) Taking many vacations is a bad thing.
(E) The media consciously misinforms the public about inequality.

10. The author lists the benefits of inequality in the third paragraph to:

(A) Create a distorted picture of the issue of wealth allocation that will lend support to an erroneous conclusion about inequality.
(B) Offend the reader and create a distraction that will hide the serious flaws in the reasoning process through which inequality is not just accepted, but justified.
(C) Call into question commonly held beliefs about the wealthy and the management of society's resources.
(D) Articulate a view about how the wealthy expend resources that will lend support to the author's suggested course of action.
(E) Offer reasoning that, while questionable, is nonetheless plausible if you accept certain of the author's assumptions.

11. The views expressed in this passage are most beneficial to:

(A) Skilled people who can convince policymakers that they will use their skills to create substantial wealth if they are given much wealth.
(B) People with wealth who try to generate substantial wealth with the resources that they currently have.
(C) Poor people because they benefit the most from policies that attempt to increase the wealth for all humanity.
(D) Middle-class people because if they follow the views in this passage they will spend their money on things that really matter.
(E) Wealthy people, because the passage justifies inequality and thereby empowers wealthy people to accumulate more wealth.

12. The primary purpose of the passage is to:

(A) Explain why there are not many things that can be done to increase humanity's wealth.
(B) Describe factors that should be considered by policymakers making decisions about wealth allocation.
(C) Criticize the way in which wealth allocation is thought of by most people who read the media.
(D) Further the interests of wealthy skilled people who take credit for advances that would have been made anyway.
(E) Boost the amount of money that everyone can spend by postulating a formula for wealth allocation that the government can follow.

GO OVER TO THE NEXT PAGE.

The welfare of women has not necessarily increased over time according to the findings of Dr. Norma Casper. While the earnings and career opportunities of women have generally increased in the industrialized world, the demands on women have also increased. For women to have a career, they must obtain an education. The time and money that they must expend to simply graduate from some of the most glamorous careers, such as law and medicine, is substantial. Most women do not get married or have a family during the time they study for such professions. After they graduate, those professions become even more demanding.

Dr. Casper believes that the "progress" that has been made by women has only furthered the interests of men. Because there are more women doctors, the quality of medical care is higher and its cost is lower than it would be otherwise. Women have not been compensated for those increases in welfare, and have in fact made deep sacrifices. As a practical matter, women doctors often cannot have children, or do not have as many children and leisure time as they would have had otherwise, because of the time pressures imposed by their profession.

While the status of women in industrialized nations is somewhat complex, it is clear that in the rest of the world women continue to be abused. For the most part, women have not been allowed to participate in professions that are respected and that are pathways to power. The effect of having a weak legal system means that physical violence against women occurs with no consequence.

A solution to this situation is complicated by the fact that women themselves are often the biggest perpetrators of the injustice that they suffer from. In a survey by Dr. Casper, a majority of women indicated that they look to men for leadership in their romantic relationships. The oppressed thus reinforce the power of the oppressors. What is remarkable is that this oppression has existed for as long as there have been historical records. Nowhere has there ever been a free society that can serve as a model for the treatment of women. Studying the welfare of men is not helpful because, even though men have for the most part been free, their freedom has been obtained at the expense of women. Men, women, and history do not provide even a starting point for formulating an approach that would increase the welfare of women. Even if such an approach were found, it could not be implemented because men are in control and will not cede that control. This is especially true of approaches that have been formulated without the input of men.

Most sociologists find Dr. Casper's studies disturbing. They believe the findings are not scientific because Dr. Casper does not assign a numerical value to the postponement of marriage and other matters that the findings identify as "sacrifices."

13. The author would most likely agree with this statement:

(A) A distribution of wealth that follows innovative techniques for identifying deserving women that have succeeded in professions.
(B) Discrimination against women by men is the primary reason humanity is not as well off as it could be.
(C) Many women have had their views about equality influenced adversely by men and by a history of the past that distorts the welfare of women.
(D) Men do not realize the burdens they place on women when they expect so many things from them.
(E) Even well-intentioned people can be oppressive towards themselves if they do not have the right guidance.

14. The passage indicates that the current condition of women is the product of:

(A) A long process that, while not completely understood because of its ubiquity, is widely accepted.
(B) Misconceptions about progress that have in fact lead to the overall decline in social welfare and the disintegration of the family.
(C) A calculated and coordinated effort by men to maintain their social status at the expense of others, including women.
(D) The hope that women could achieve freedom by engaging in the oppressive acts that have brought men a measure of freedom.
(E) A system in which the condition of women is sought to be improved by industrializing nations so that they have more wealth.

GO OVER TO THE NEXT PAGE.

15. The author includes the views of most sociologists to:

(A) discredit Dr. Casper
(B) give a balanced view
(C) show an alternative approach
(D) highlight an issue
(E) qualify Dr. Casper's comparisons

16. The author's main purpose is to:

(A) expose the shortcomings of a radical theory by giving a number of examples in which it doesn't work and by explaining why it does not follow acceptable analytical steps for modern scientific inquiry.
(B) explore avenues for formulating an acceptable theory of social equality by describing shortcomings of the historical approach and the current approach taken by other theories.
(C) help women and encourage social change by reporting the highlights of significant and groundbreaking research that calls into question our basic understanding of the world.
(D) describe, with the help of scholarly research, how a number of commonly held views of women are not true and give a number of examples to support that conclusion.
(E) showcase Dr. Casper's finding that it is not possible to find a solution to the adverse treatment of women by using the scientific method, studying history, or other common approaches.

17. The purpose of the second paragraph is to:

(A) show how the medical profession in particular abuses women
(B) explain how an apparent good thing has in fact produced bad consequences
(C) indicate how the male conspiracy to oppress women has infiltrated an admired profession
(D) give an example of a failed approach in which even intelligent people were misled
(E) lay a factual basis from which a solution to the problem will naturally follow

18. Dr. Casper probably believes that:

(A) A solution to the problem she has studied is difficult to arrive at for more than one reason.
(B) It is not important to articulate her findings in numerical terms.
(C) If women were better off, everyone would be better off.
(D) Leadership is a form of wealth when it comes to comparing genders.
(E) Women should take responsibility for their actions by not getting into bad situations.

19. Under the reasoning in the passage, the relationship between men and women can best be described as:

(A) troubled, because women have not taken the initiative to do what is right for them
(B) damaged beyond repair because of long lasting discord
(C) less beneficial for women than it should be in light of what women do
(D) complicated such that unraveling its intricacies is probably not helpful
(E) something that may improve as technology advances

GO OVER TO THE NEXT PAGE.

A political action group called Green Citizens is proposing legislation that would change how rights to water from the Clear Blue River would be allocated. Currently, farmers along the river use the water to irrigate their fields. Each farmer has a right to a certain amount of water that is based on the size of their property. If a farmer does not use their total water allotment, then nobody is allowed the use of the unused amount. This system has existed for several decades and is critical to the continuing success of the stable farm community along the river.

The Green Citizens have identified a number of problems with this system, and claim that those problems would be solved with a system in which rights to water are sold to the highest bidder. Of particular concern for the Citizens is their belief that the water can be more productively used for things other than farming. Water taken out of the river for irrigation lowers the level of the river. Some of that water washes back into the river with high concentrations of pesticides. The river is thus not able to have the wildlife that it would have without irrigation. If the rights to that water could be sold, the Citizens would buy them to enable wildlife to flourish in the river.

Farmers along the river are divided on the Citizens' proposed legislation. Some believe that the sale of their water rights will generate a substantial amount of money. They could use such money to invest in businesses that do not require irrigation. Other farmers are opposed to the legislation because they believe it will destabilize their community. These farmers are concerned that over time a substantial number of farmers along the river will sell the rights to their water. If that happens, farming will cease to be a viable business for the remaining farmers. Dealerships for farming equipment, and other businesses that support the farming industry, will no longer operate in the area because there will not be a critical mass necessary for such businesses.

In an unusual alliance, real estate developers have joined forces with the Green Citizens. These developers see a unique opportunity that would be created if the legislation passes. If the land along the river no longer had rights to the water, that land would be cheaper. If the river had more water, and thus more wildlife, it would be a more attractive place for people to live on its banks. Subdivisions could be placed along the river and the homes in them could be sold at a substantial profit. The developers would need to purchase some water permits to supply water to their developments, but those water needs would not be as much as is needed to irrigate the same amount of land.

Clear Blue University has performed a study on the probable effects of the proposed legislation, the conclusion of which is that the legislation is unnecessary. The developers could achieve their purposes by simply buying the existing land, using some of the water for residential purposes, and leaving the remaining water to nourish the wildlife.

20. The author would most likely agree with which of these statements:

(A) farming is not as productive as it once was along the river
(B) a new system for allocating water may be beneficial, but must be closely studied
(C) the correct solution will not be enacted because most voters are not farmers
(D) development of land along the river would only be marginally beneficial
(E) the current system should be kept because the proposed legislation will not change anything

21. If the legislation passes and a large industrial corporation buys a substantial amount of water rights for use in an activity that will pollute the river more than the current farming industry does, which of the following is the most persuasive reason for enjoining such activity through a court proceeding?

(A) The industrial activity will have a negative impact on land values along the river.
(B) Wildlife and farmers down river will be adversely affected by the pollution.
(C) Developers will have a harder time profiting from the sale of homes along the river.
(D) The pollution will be disruptive to the stable farm community that depends on the river.
(E) The purpose of the legislation was to reduce pollution, not to enable more pollution.

GO OVER TO THE NEXT PAGE.

22. The passage supports the following conclusions about the river, EXCEPT:

(A) It is a significant factor that affects the current and potential wellbeing of the economy of the land that it runs through.
(B) Wildlife that depends on the river can be protected under the current legal framework that establishes water rights.
(C) It is possible that the water in the river is not as pure as it should be when the welfare of the wildlife and the surrounding community are all taken into account.
(D) The full economic potential of the river may not be realized if the water rights are not separated from the ownership rights of the land along the river.
(E) The existing farming community should be preserved, even if that means that other beneficial activities by the river must be foregone.

23. The passage establishes which of the following with respect to the Green Citizens:

(A) They are a group of narrow minded people who do not have a stake in the existing economy that depends on the river.
(B) Skepticism with respect to their approach is proper because they have taken on an issue that is more complex than they realize.
(C) Its members are selfish because they want to change the river water rights in a manner that is beneficial to them, regardless of the consequences.
(D) They seek to implement change in a manner that does not force existing stakeholders to give up their rights in the short term.
(E) Development is something that should generally be opposed because restoring nature to its original condition is a higher goal.

24. The author included in the last paragraph to:

(A) call into question the usefulness of the proposed legislation
(B) indicate that the developers are dishonest in their support of the legislation
(C) critique the reasoning of the Green Citizens
(D) outline an alternative approach that others have not considered
(E) challenge assumptions of the legislation in light of conditions along the river

25. The author's attitude towards the proposed legislation is most accurately described as:

(A) convinced that it will pass, but cautious about whether it will be helpful
(B) convinced that it will pass, but not supportive of its goals
(C) largely indifferent towards the legislation, and sympathetic towards the farmers
(D) convinced that it will not pass, but hopeful that a better solution will be found
(E) convinced that it will not pass, and indifferent towards the consequences of it not passing

26. Which of the following questions is answered by the passage?

(A) Which crops are grown along the river?
(B) Can homes be built along the river?
(C) Will the legislation on balance be beneficial?
(D) Are some farmers part of Green Citizens?
(E) What is the best water level for the river?

S T O P

35 minutes

1. Gina: this lot is desolate. We should clear the rocks from it and plant hardy trees. Then it will no longer be desolate.

Peter: Even hardy trees cannot withstand the harsh climate here. The lot will once again become desolate if the trees are not planted properly and cared for regularly.

Peter tells Gina that:

(A) A good part of a plan will not automatically produce the desired result.
(B) The proper method here does not necessarily apply to other landscaping projects.
(C) The logical approach is not necessarily obvious.
(D) There is more than one way to accomplish a task.
(E) Some solutions are counterproductive.

2. The standard of living in Bigville has steadily increased over the past ten years even though the annual income of its residents has declined over the same period of time.

Which of the following can describe the apparent discrepancy above?

(A) Advances in technology have created conveniences people only dreamed of ten years ago.
(B) The number of residents in Bigville has declined over the past ten years.
(C) Annual income is only one factor that determines a city's standard of living.
(D) Over the past ten years the annual income in the rest of the country has declined more than it has in Bigville.
(E) Methods for calculating standard of living have changed over time.

3. All red wines from Hinterton Valley have higher acidity levels and are more popular than cheaper wines from Cantor Valley. Most Hinterton Valley white wines cost more than Cantor Valley white wines, but none of them cost as much as Cantor Valley red wines. Sparkling white wines from both valleys are cheaper than any other wine from their valley of origin.

Joseph Price, a wine that is cheaper than some Cantor Valley white wines, could be:

(A) The cheapest Cantor Valley sparkling wine.
(B) A red wine from Hinterton Valley.
(C) A Hinterton Valley white wine.
(D) The most expensive Cantor Valley red wine.
(E) A Hinterton Valley sparkling wine.

GO OVER TO THE NEXT PAGE.

4. Congress will not pass recently introduced legislation that simplifies taxes on homes because that legislation does not enjoy popular support. Most of the respondents in a nationwide survey of homeowners indicated that they oppose legislation that would change how their homes are taxed, even if their overall tax rate would remain the same.

Which of the following is an assumption upon which the above reasoning depends?

  (A) The survey accurately identified a group of voters who can establish whether the legislation has popular support.
  (B) The respondents to the nationwide survey hold views that are representative of all homeowners.
  (C) The survey is valid because people who oppose changing legislation also oppose simplifying legislation.
  (D) The survey was accurate.
  (E) The legislature will enact only legislation that has popular support.

5. It is preferable to own a young pet turtle that will live for a long time than to have a pet dog because the lifespan of a dog is substantially shorter than that of a human being. If you have a pet dog, it is likely that you will go through the grief of witnessing your pet grow old and eventually die.

The above reasoning is most closely paralleled by the argument that:

  (A) It is best to own healthy animals because they are more fun.
  (B) It is okay to live a selfish life because you only live once.
  (C) If dogs lived longer they would be better pets.
  (D) Diamond rings are preferable to cars because they last longer.
  (E) Elderly humans should own dogs instead of turtles.

6. Critic: You invest only in tanker companies that have double hulled tankers to help protect wildlife when there is an oil spill. However, those same companies also have single hulled tankers that represent a serious threat to seals, otters, and several kinds of fish. If you are serious about protecting wildlife, you should not invest in those companies.

If valid, which of these principles would most support the critic's position?

  (A) It is better to directly help a cause than to indirectly hurt such cause, even if you receive some personal benefit.
  (B) You should place your resources only in organizations that always act to further things you're serious about.
  (C) Some compromises are inevitably necessary, especially with regard to large organizations.
  (D) If a group of creatures is unable to protect itself, you should do your part to help those creatures survive.
  (E) Helping the helpless is far more rewarding than profiting from an activity that can potentially hurt the helpless.

7. Certain of the ball bearings from X Co. are flawed. It follows that, because it is of critical importance that the space station function with a minimal amount of mechanical breakdowns, no bearings from X Co. should be used on the space station.

This argument is flawed because it:

  (A) Does not distinguish between a necessary outcome and an acceptable outcome.
  (B) Confuses a spatial relationship for a causal one.
  (C) Assumes that a better result can be obtained with another approach.
  (D) Establishes a causal connection where such connection does not necessarily exist.
  (E) Draws a conclusion based on what could be isolated cases.

GO OVER TO THE NEXT PAGE.

8. The bug population in farmer Rodriguez' crops has declined consistently over the past three years despite the fact that pests in the Benitez valley, where the farm is located, have increased over the same period of time. Clearly, Mr. Rodriguez is a better farmer than his colleagues in the Benitez valley.

The above reasoning assumes:

(A) Mr. Rodriguez was responsible for the decline in the bug population of his crops.
(B) The crops grown by Mr. Rodriguez are similar to the rest of the crops grown in Benitez valley.
(C) The areas of the Benitez valley that experienced an increase in pests were farmland.
(D) Pest control, and not crop production, is a more important factor in determining whether someone is a good farmer.
(E) A decline in bug population is good, even if it is accomplished with harmful pesticides.

9. The discrepancy in bug populations can be explained by the fact that:

(A) In the past three years Mr. Rodriguez has planted different crops that are not hospitable to the bugs in the valley.
(B) Mr. Rodriguez is a good person.
(C) Mr. Rodriguez' crops yield more than those of his colleagues in the valley.
(D) The land on Mr. Rodriguez' farm is more fertile than other land in the valley.
(E) Genetically engineered crops grow despite the presence of pests.

10. Human beings possess an intuitive sense of the truth. A recent study has found that this sense of the truth extends beyond basic concepts, such as the widespread belief that murder is wrong. The study found that people were able to discern whether some facts were true when a person informed them, in a monotone voice, of various true and untrue facts.

The above argument is most strengthened by which of the following:

(A) The participants in the study were smart older people with extensive experience dealing with life issues.
(B) The results of the study were more mixed when it came to the participants' ability to discern half truths.
(C) Other studies performed on higher level primates have come to similar conclusions, albeit the truths used were simpler.
(D) A similar study arrived at a similar conclusion when participants were informed of true and untrue information through a loudspeaker.
(E) Most people are affected by a truth when they are able to discern it through their own intuition, and not when the truth is explained to them.

11. The electric utility sought to justify the 10 percent increase in utility rates by indicating that most of the increase was necessary because of the need to develop alternative forms of energy generation, such as solar energy. But, a careful analysis of the utility's expenditures shows that solar energy has, and will continue to be, a small part of the budget. Overhead costs and expenditures on coal and gas remained significant parts of the utility's budget. The utility's justification is not credible.

If true, which of the following most strengthens the conclusion that the utility's justification is not credible?

(A) This year most utilities are increasing their budget by at least 10 percent.
(B) Gas prices have increased substantially and are expected to continue to increase.
(C) It is not cost-effective to develop solar energy at this time because the technology is too undeveloped.
(D) In the past, the utility has tried to use improper justifications for rate increases.
(E) The "overhead expenses" being increased include the salary paid to the CEO.

GO OVER TO THE NEXT PAGE.

12. Principal: Students learn everything they know about biology from their biology professor. Thus, no student will know more than any other student if the biology professor teaches everyone effectively. If no student is more knowledgeable than other students, no student can do better than the other students. But an effective professor does not teach everything there is to know about biology. Therefore some students can know more than the rest of the students.

Which of the following explains the apparent conflict in the principal's statements?

(A) The principal is unreasonable and the conflict cannot be explained.
(B) There is no conflict because the principal is describing the initial stages in how students acquire information.
(C) The statements do not account for differences in intelligence between students and in their level of interest in biology.
(D) The principal does not consider the possibility that certain biology professors teach more biology than others and that certain environments are more biologically diverse than others.
(E) As long as an effective professor is the only source of biology information, no student will have an advantage, but that changes as students access other information sources.

13. Mr. Jones, the mayor of Pleasantville, wants to raise taxes to pay for a golden statue commemorating his achievements. Taxes should be raised to pay for more worthy causes, not to fund a useless pork-barrel project.

This argument would be weakened if:

(A) A public project's merit is determined by how popular it is, and Pleasantville supports a statute of Mr. Jones.
(B) Some of Mr. Jones' achievements have included the construction statues of famous people.
(C) Hungry homeless children are the single biggest issue facing Pleasantville.
(D) Pleasantville is a highly prosperous town that can easily afford higher taxes.
(E) A statue of Mr. Jones is a worthy cause because he is a good person.

14. From 1992 to 1996 a state program was in place under which university applicants who identified themselves as Native Americans received a substantial subsidy. During those years the number of applicants who identified themselves as Native Americans tripled, and they were enrolled in university programs at the same rate as other applicants. However, there was no increase in student participation with respect to activities commonly associated with Native Americans, such as courses on the history of Native Americans, student groups devoted to addressing Native American issues, etc. After 1996 participation in those kinds of activities remained roughly in line with what it had been during the prior decade, even though applicants identifying themselves as Native Americans declined substantially.

Which of these statements is the strongest conclusion that can be made with respect to the above information?

(A) While student participation in university programs was subsidized, Native American programs were not, and thus the new applicants found them uninteresting.
(B) It is difficult to arrive at a conclusion about participation in Native American programs because there is no clear definition of who is "Native American."
(C) The subsidy program was flawed because it simply required applicants to identify their ethnic origin, without additional proof of their origin.
(D) The subsidy program was unfair towards other disadvantaged minorities because it did not allocate any funds to those groups.
(E) The increase in Native American applicants was made up of people who were not Native American, or who are not commonly thought of as such.

GO OVER TO THE NEXT PAGE.

15. A government program to reduce pollution offers car owners the fair market value of their cars if they have emissions of pollutants that are above a certain threshold. The car owners also get a tax deduction for the amount that their vehicle is purchased for. Bob planned on taking his old and highly polluting vehicle to a junkyard and dispose of it, but instead he sold the vehicle to the government under the program. With the money he bought a large SUV that pollutes more than a vehicle he would have purchased without the money from the government.

If the above is true, the government program must:

(A) have been enacted for the wrong reasons because it does not benefit the government or the environment.
(B) be changed so that people who are thinking about junking their vehicles do not get money from the government.
(C) create more pollution in certain circumstances than would exist had the program not been enacted.
(D) be repealed because, rather than lowering pollution, it actually increases the level of pollution emitted by cars.
(E) impose a penalty on Bob because he is unfairly taking advantage of a situation that he has contributed to.

16. John: Obeying the speed limit is of no value. Even if we had obeyed the speed limit we would still have been involved in the accident by the big bend last year. The speed limit does not address the root problems of highway safety.

Margret: Any rule that could possibly help drivers is useful. The speed limit prevents certain crashes. Whenever a crash occurs there is a potential for people to be injured and property to be damaged.

Margret indicates:

(A) The speed limit's utility should be evaluated in light of additional considerations.
(B) There are other reasons why last year's accident could have been avoided.
(C) The proper speed limit in one case may be used in other cases.
(D) John incorrectly assumes that driving a different speed would have avoided last year's accident.
(E) John fails to take into account an important distinction between actual usefulness and possible usefulness.

17. Tall people, who society routinely rewards with influential positions, do not appreciate the difficulties shorter people face. Studies have found that most women want to date men who are taller than themselves. It is not a coincidence that Abraham Lincoln was a tall person because voters tend to elect tall officials. Society does a disservice to itself by giving weight to an arbitrary feature that people have no control over and that bears no connection to the task of performing the duties of influential positions.

The above conclusion depends on the following assumption:

(A) People's interests are served when a person's ability to perform a duty is given weight, regardless of people's preferences.
(B) Society should give other characteristics, such as a person's accomplishments, more weight.
(C) Short people are as capable as tall people.
(D) Most tall people are appointed to positions for which they are not qualified.
(E) There probably was a shorter person who could have been a better president than Abraham Lincoln.

GO OVER TO THE NEXT PAGE.

18. Teacher: the deepest truths are often the most obvious ones, which people do not acknowledge because they are also inconvenient truths.

Which of the following principles most closely conforms to the principle expressed above?

    (A) Solutions to exam questions may be placed in an exam itself because people will not read them anyway, even if they do not know the answer to an exam question.

    (B) Some of the best solutions to poverty, such as honest government, are not implemented because they are not in everyone's interests.

    (C) If you take time to stop and think of the many good things you have, you will be more grateful and have a better understanding of what you should do with your life.

    (D) The best inventions that have been made occurred because an inventor took a seemingly ordinary object and turned it into something extraordinary.

    (E) Pain can be a professor if, through discernment, you carefully examine difficult situations of the past and gain strength from them for the future.

19. Politician: The use of military force is appropriate when only the aggressor feels the effects of such force. Military force is not appropriate when it affects innocent people and when it is expensive.

Which of the following is most supported by the position articulated by the politician?

    (A) The invasion of country A impacted most, but not all, the aggressors. Therefore, if it was not expensive, it was appropriate.

    (B) The invasion of country Q impacted only a few aggressors and was expensive. It was therefore inappropriate.

    (C) The use of military force in country S is highly expensive. If it does not affect aggressors, it is inappropriate.

    (D) The use of military force in country B was inexpensive, but did not affect many aggressors. Therefore it was not appropriate.

    (E) Sending troops to the capital of country X affected only aggressors and no innocent people. It was thus appropriate.

20. John: I oppose the death penalty because killing people is immoral, no matter what the circumstances.

Peter: I support the death penalty because sometimes it is necessary to execute people to save other lives.

John's argument would be strengthened if:

    (A) It is not humanly possible to determine when lives can be saved by killing people.

    (B) Most people believe that killing people is immoral.

    (C) The death penalty has never, in fact, saved lives.

    (D) Even with advances in DNA science, people are still mistakenly given the death penalty.

    (E) Giving people a life sentence is sufficient punishment for even the worst of crimes.

GO OVER TO THE NEXT PAGE.

21. Most people from infancy have one main language that they speak. When they learn another language they invariably speak that language with the accent of their first language. In today's globalized economy, many people are beginning to speak two languages throughout their formative years. When they learn a third language they usually speak it with less of an accent, even if the language is not related to the family of languages of their first two languages.

From the information above one can most strongly conclude that:

(A) People who know only one language in their formative years are not as motivated as others to learn another language.
(B) People who know two languages are smarter than people who know only one language.
(C) Knowing three languages in your formative years makes language acquisition even easier.
(D) Knowing two languages well can help people to communicate in a third language.
(E) If you know only one language, the best way to learn a hard language is to first learn an easier one.

22. Teacher: The head coach of the most successful football team in the state told me that his best players studied football strategies in class. Therefore, to make our team better I suggest that we have them attend football classes.

All of the following would, if true, weaken the teacher's reasoning about the football classes EXCEPT:

(A) Football strategies are best taught on the football field during practice.
(B) Morale of a game is important for winning and sitting in a class hurts a football team's morale.
(C) While some players improve in class, most football positions simply require brute force.
(D) Most football teachers have a limited understanding of how strategies are implemented.
(E) Taking football classes is an interesting and stimulating activity for most teams.

23. Traffic on the winding two lane Taterbed road through the Pierlight mountain pass is always congested because large slow trucks do not allow faster cars to safely pass. The road would be much safer if it were widened to four lanes.

Which of the following is an assumption upon which the above reasoning depends?

(A) It is possible for cars to drive through the Pierlight pass at both higher speeds and in a safer manner.
(B) The Taterbed road will be safer if it is less congested.
(C) It is possible to widen the Taterbed road to four lanes.
(D) More cars and trucks will not travel on the Taterbed road if it is widened to four lanes.
(E) Roads with more lanes are safer.

24. Critic: None of the several witnesses to the recent gas truck collision are credible because they each have a different opinion as to the cause of the accident. The witnesses are either trying to further their own agenda, or they were not paying attention when the accident occurred. Thus, they are not reliable.

The critic's argument is flawed because:

(A) There are other reasons that could explain why the witnesses have different opinions about such an accident.
(B) It concludes, based on a difference as to one aspect of the crash, that the witnesses are entirely not credible.
(C) It is insensitive to the fact that the accident may have been traumatic and thus affected the perceptions of the witnesses.
(D) If the witnesses' opinions are not taken into account, we will not have a full picture of what occurred in the accident.
(E) The uncertainties caused by the inconsistent accounts could be reconciled by using physical evidence from the crash.

GO OVER TO THE NEXT PAGE.

96

25. Journalists believe multinationals are taking advantage of the labor force in Province X. This is an erroneous view because most people believe journalists' views about multinationals are mistaken.

The conclusion can be critiqued because:

(A) The phrase "taking advantage" is unclear.
(B) Journalists as a group do not have cohesive views.
(C) The author arrives at the conclusion based only upon the view of "most people."
(D) The conclusion is based on the assumption that journalists cannot properly evaluate a situation.
(E) It assumes that what is true of one multinational is true of all of them.

26. Mr. Lozano, a high profile artist from Bolivia, has four basic kinds of subject matter that he paints: landscapes, seascapes, birds and cars. He also places either men or women in his paintings, but not both. A museum curator has also observed that Mr. Lozano always places women in his paintings of birds.

Which of the following must be true about Mr. Lozano's art if the above statements are true?

(A) If Mr. Lozano does a painting of birds, he does not place men in the painting.
(B) Mr. Lozano's paintings of cars do not have women in them.
(C) None of the artist's paintings combine seascapes and birds.
(D) If men are in a painting, then its subject matter is either cars or landscapes.
(E) The artist would benefit by significantly expanding the range of his subject matter.

S T O P

35 minutes

Mary uses only six spices when she cooks: cumin, salt, basil, paprika, oregano and cinnamon. Her culinary rules only allow her to use the spices as follows:
Basil and paprika cannot be used together.
Basil and cumin cannot be used together.
When Mary uses oregano, she cannot also use paprika, cumin or basil.

1.   Which of these could Mary use together:

   (A) paprika and cumin
   (B) oregano and cumin
   (C) basil and cumin
   (D) basil and paprika
   (E) oregano and paprika

2.   If Mary is not using salt or cinnamon, but is using two spices, which of the following is all of the spices Mary CANNOT use?

   (A) oregano
   (B) basil
   (C) oregano and basil
   (D) paprika and cumin
   (E) basil and paprika

3.   Mary CANNOT use:

   (A) salt and oregano
   (B) paprika and cumin
   (C) oregano while using three other spices
   (D) basil while using two other spices
   (E) cumin while using three other spices

4.   Mary must use:

   (A) at most, three other spices when using oregano
   (B) at most, five spices
   (C) salt with at least one other spice
   (D) at most, three spices
   (E) at most, four spices

5.   If Mary uses two spices, what are the total number of combinations she could be using?

   (A) 9
   (B) 10
   (C) 12
   (D) 7
   (E) 14

6.   If Mary is not allowed to use less than a total of three spices under her rules, which of the following must be true:

   (A) Mary is using salt and cumin.
   (B) Mary is not using oregano.
   (C) Mary is using cinnamon, but not basil.
   (D) Mary is using paprika or cumin.
   (E) Mary is using salt, or cinnamon, or both salt and cinnamon.

GO OVER TO THE NEXT PAGE.

A teacher tutors nine children: B, F, H, I, N, P, R, S, and V. The children are tutored one at a time, once a day. Each child is tutored in one sitting. The teacher teaches the children according to the following rules:

S and V are both taught before H.
N and B are both taught before P.
R is taught after P, but before F.
I is taught at some point before F.

7. It is possible that:

(A) F is the fifth person taught.
(B) N is the seventh person taught.
(C) B is the eighth person taught.
(D) I is the eighth person taught.
(E) P is the ninth person taught.

8. If H is taught fourth, any of the following could be taught third, EXCEPT:

(A) I
(B) R
(C) B
(D) N
(E) V

9. Which child CANNOT be taught fourth?

(A) R
(B) H
(C) P
(D) B
(E) F

10. If F is taught sixth, then which of the following must be correct?

(A) S is taught seventh.
(B) I is taught fifth.
(C) H is taught ninth.
(D) N is taught first.
(E) P is taught third.

11. If S is the sixth person that is taught, which of these must be correct?

(A) H is taught after P.
(B) V is taught before F.
(C) I is taught after R.
(D) R is taught before V.
(E) N is taught after B.

12. If V is taught fifth, which one of these could be correct?

(A) N is taught after R.
(B) V is taught before B.
(C) H is taught before N.
(D) P is taught after H.
(E) F is taught right after V.

GO OVER TO THE NEXT PAGE.

Four general practitioners – Drs. Barnerdale, Eavedorn, Artnarp, and Coopersman -- and three specialists -- Drs. Marstervel, Ostwawill, and Partnit each see patients once a day in one of two clinics – Arsbald and Bodt. Each doctor sees patients for exactly one half hour. The clinics are right next to each other and are open for patient visits only during these times: Arsbald at 1 p.m., 1:30 p.m. and 2 p.m., and Bodt at 1:30 p.m., 2 p.m., 2:30 p.m. and 3 p.m.

The doctors see their patients according to these rules:

Dr. Barnerdale sees patients right before a specialist, but not necessarily in the same clinic.

Drs. Coopersman and Ostwawill see patients in different clinics.

If a specialist sees someone at 1:30 p.m., no general practitioner sees anyone at that time.

Dr. Artnarp sees patients at some point in time before Dr. Eavedorn.

Dr. Coopersman sees patients at either 1 p.m. or 3 p.m.

13. If a specialist sees a patient at 1:30 p.m. then which of these must be true?

   (A) Coopersman cannot be in a time slot right before Ostwawill.
   (B) Barnerdale must see patients at 2 p.m.
   (C) Artnarp cannot be scheduled at 1 p.m.
   (D) Barnerdale cannot schedule patients at 2:30 p.m.
   (E) Marstervel and Partnit must be scheduled at 1:30 p.m.

14. If Barnerdale sees patients at 1 p.m. which could be a proper scheduling of doctors at Bodt from 1:30 p.m. to 2: 30 p.m.?

   (A) Marstervel, Partnit, Eavedorn
   (B) Marstervel, Eavedorn, Partnit
   (C) Ostwawill, Artnarp, Eavedorn
   (D) Artnarp, Eavedorn, Partnit
   (E) Eavedorn, Marstervel, Partnit

15. Which doctors must see patients before 2:30 p.m.?

   (A) Coopersman and Artnarp
   (B) Ostwawill and Barnerdale
   (C) Coopersman and Partnit
   (D) Marstervel and Ostwawill
   (E) Barnerdale and Artnarp

16. Which of these could be the schedule for Arsbald?

   (A) Artnarp, Eavedorn, Partnit
   (B) Coopersman, Partnit, Barnerdale
   (C) Marstervel, Partnit and Ostwawill
   (D) Ostwawill, Marstervel and Artnarp
   (E) Barnerdale, Ostwawill and Eavedorn

17. Which doctors may see patients at 2:30 p.m. if Partnit is scheduled at 3 p.m. and if Eavedorn must see patients right after Artnarp?

   (A) Barnerdale
   (B) Artnarp
   (C) Eavedorn
   (D) Coopersman
   (E) Ostwawill

18. If Barnerdale sees patients at 2 p.m., which of the following must be true?

   (A) Eavedorn sees patients at 2 p.m.
   (B) A specialist cannot see patients at 3 p.m.
   (C) Coopersman sees patients at 3 p.m.
   (D) Barnerdale sees patients in Bodt.
   (E) Ostwawill sees patients at 2:30 p.m.

GO OVER TO THE NEXT PAGE.

Seven teachers teach in a vocational school: Ronald, Steve, Valerie, Wayne, Zeba, Alice and Marcia. Each teacher teaches one or more of these four classes: woodworking, auto repair, bricklaying and electronics.

They teach according to these conditions:

Valerie and only four other teachers teach bricklaying.

Steve teaches electronics and woodworking.

Alice doesn't teach any course that Steve teaches.

Marcia teaches more kinds of classes than Steve.

Zeba doesn't teach any course that Alice teaches.

Ronald teaches exactly three courses.

19. Which teachers can teach exactly the same courses as each other?

(A) Marcia and Alice
(B) Marcia and Steve
(C) Alice and Wayne
(D) Steve and Alice
(E) Alice and Ronald

20. Which of these must be correct?

(A) Ronald and Marcia teach the same courses, but neither of them teach bricklaying.
(B) Steve and Alice teach the same courses, but neither teaches auto repair.
(C) Valerie and Wayne teach bricklaying and auto repair, but not electronics or woodworking.
(D) Alice teaches either auto repair, or bricklaying, or both auto repair and bricklaying.
(E) Ronald and Steve teach the same number of courses, but do not teach bricklaying

21. Which of these cannot be correct?

(A) Valerie teaches two courses.
(B) Ronald and Steve teach woodworking.
(C) Alice and Steve teach the same number of courses.
(D) Marcia teaches as many courses as Ronald.
(E) Marcia teaches as many courses as Alice

22. Wayne must teach:

(A) at least two classes
(B) bricklaying
(C) all courses that Valerie teaches
(D) electronics
(E) at least two classes that Marcia teaches

23. Which of the following is a complete list of all teachers who can teach all courses?

(A) Valerie, Wayne, Marcia
(B) Marcia and Wayne
(C) Valerie, Wayne, Marcia, Steve
(D) Zeba, Valerie, Wayne, Marcia
(E) Alice, Ronald, Valerie

S T O P

Appendix E

Answer Key

SECTION I: LOGICAL REASONING		SECTION II: READING COMPREHENSION		SECTION III: LOGICAL REASONING		SECTION IV: LOGIC GAMES	
1.	A	1.	E	1.	A	1.	A
2.	B	2.	B	2.	C	2.	C
3.	E	3.	D	3.	E	3.	C
4.	A	4.	A	4.	A	4.	E
5.	D	5.	B	5.	D	5.	B
6.	B	6.	E	6.	B	6.	E
7.	C	7.	B	7.	E	7.	D
8.	A	8.	C	8.	A	8.	B
9.	B	9.	C	9.	A	9.	E
10.	C	10.	D	10.	D	10.	C
11.	D	11.	A	11.	B	11.	A
12.	A	12.	B	12.	E	12.	D
13.	C	13.	C	13.	A	13.	D
14.	B	14.	A	14.	E	14.	A
15.	D	15.	E	15.	C	15.	E
16.	A	16.	D	16.	A	16.	B
17.	C	17.	B	17.	A	17.	E
18.	B	18.	A	18.	B	18.	B
19.	A	19.	C	19.	C	19.	C
20.	E	20.	B	20.	A	20.	D
21.	A	21.	E	21.	D	21.	E
22.	B	22.	E	22.	E	22.	B
23.	C	23.	D	23.	A	23.	A
24.	A	24.	A	24.	B		
25.	B	25.	C	25.	C		
26.	C	26.	B	26.	A		

SECTION I: LOGICAL REASONING

1.   The facts in this question about the Slenderhead are found in the first three sentences. The author then concludes "The State has acted irresponsibly by endangering the future of the Slenderhead in Spear Lake." This conclusion is not directly supported by the facts. The facts do not say the powerplant will endanger the Slenderhead. But, the plant will probably have an effect on the fish because it will lower the amount of oxygen in the water. The author of assumes the lower oxygen level will endanger the fish. Answer choice A states that assumption.

Answer choice B is incorrect because it is too extreme. Whether there is "only" one way for the State to act responsibly is not germane to this question. Choice C is not relevant because the question concerns the future of the Slenderhead *in Spear Lake*. Choice D is incorrect because the author does not make a conclusion about whether the Slenderhead species will survive. The author is only concerned with the Slenderhead's existence in Spear Lake. Choice E is incorrect because it is too broad. The question does not concern wildlife in general. It concerns the Slenderhead. Whether the Federal government is responsible for wildlife does not have a bearing on how lower oxygen levels will affect the Slenderhead in Spear Lake.

2.   Answer choice B is correct because it attacks a critical connection that is necessary for the argument. The argument connects fatigue in the muscles of the heart to a risk of heart failure. By detecting the fatigue, the reasoning concludes that we can detect the risk of heart failure. However, if there is no connection between fatigue and heart failure, the reasoning falls apart. Answer choice A is incorrect because the reasoning is not dependent on people's awareness of heart fatigue. Answer choice C is incorrect because the qualities of a well-rounded astronaut are not at issue in this question. The reasoning in this question narrowly concerns avoidance of the risk of heart failure. Answer choice D is incorrect because the absence of the use of technology in the past does not indicate that in the future technology will not work. Answer choice E is incorrect because answer choice B is stronger. Even if fatigue is only one factor affecting a person's risk of heart failure, it can still be used to reduce the risk of heart failure in astronauts.

3.   Answer choice E is correct because it points out that conflict has advantages despite the bad effects conflict can have. Answer choice A is incorrect because the passage does not weigh the benefits of conflict against its adverse effects. Answer choice B is incorrect because the passage does not address the downside of not having conflict. Answer choice C is incorrect because the passage does not indicate whether, on balance, conflict is beneficial. Answer choice D is incorrect because the passage does not advocate a combination of conflict and absence of conflict. The passage simply indicates that conflict has been beneficial, along with being destructive.

4.   Choice A is correct because the author indicates that bankruptcy, which is definitely painful, should be avoided if debts can potentially be paid. B is incorrect because under these facts even hard work may not resolve a person's huge debt burden. Answer C is incorrect because there is no indication that people considering bankruptcy

are irresponsible. Choice D is incorrect because the author concedes that for some people there is no long-term solution (bankruptcy should be avoided "unless there is simply no way" to repay the debt). Choice E is wrong because the author concedes that sometimes the short term solution (bankruptcy) is the best solution to a person's heavy debt load.

5.   Answer choice A is incorrect because it is not relevant to the issue of representation on the council. B is incorrect because Mary's information adds to, and does not compete with, Chuck's data. C is incorrect because Chuck's information is made more complete with Mary's information. Its accuracy is not questioned. D is correct. Chuck did not take into account the relative size of the tribes when arriving at his conclusion. E is incorrect because Chuck has not taken into account the tribe's size, but he has not improperly defined them.

6.   Answer choice B is correct because it establishes that exercise may help accomplish one thing that a diet accomplishes, namely supplying the body with needed nutrients. Answer choice A is incorrect because it does not address a weakness in the diets, but rather in the people who are on the diets. Answer choice C is incorrect because it does not call into question the usefulness of diets themselves. Instead, it calls into question the integrity of the dieting industry. Answer choice D is incorrect because the word "diet" as used in this answer choice means to eat less. The question, however, concerns whether diets should be "the primary method of strengthening the body". Thus, this question is about gaining strength, not how to lose weight. Answer choice E is incorrect because who successful celebrities are, and what they do not promote, are not necessarily the product of a wellness routine for strengthening the body.

7.   Answer choice C is correct because it most closely articulates the student's flawed reasoning. By noting that some university graduates are not successful, the student concludes that a university degree does not create successful people. Answer choice A is incorrect because the student's reasoning does not necessarily justify lack of industriousness. Instead of attending a university, a person could do something else more productive with their life according to the reasoning of the student. Answer choice B is incorrect because the student reasoned about the usefulness of a university education, not the nature of success. Answer choice D is incorrect because it is not as strong as answer choice C. Answer choice D discusses a possible explanation for why a subset of university graduates may not be successful. Answer choice C deals with the relationship between success and education, which is at the core of the student's analysis. Answer choice E is incorrect because whether other levels of education create successful people does not have a direct bearing on whether a university education in particular will create such people.

8.   Answer choice A is correct because the passage mainly concerns the greater artistic freedom found in an art form not bound by "scenes observed in nature." Answer choices B, C and D are incorrect because the passage does not concern itself with what "good" art is. Answer choice E is incorrect because the passage concerns the qualities of Modern art.

9. A is incorrect because the author does not change the use of "cramps". B is correct. The author takes the fact that spicy food *can* cause cramps and concludes that it *must have* caused cramps. C is incorrect. The conclusion uses relevant information, although it manipulates it with flawed reasoning. D is also incorrect. The author extends a rule too far, and does not use an overbroad rule. Finally, E is incorrect. The conclusion does ignore this possibility, but that is not *why* it is vulnerable to criticism.

10. Answer choice C is correct because the author only considers the cost-effectiveness of reducing certain defects, but does not look at the cost of reducing additional defects. Answer choice A is incorrect because failure to consider a certain possibility is not the ground for which the argument is most susceptible to critique. There are many other possibilities that the author has not considered, and those possibilities are also not the strongest reason for critiquing the argument. Answer choice B is incorrect because it is not as strong as answer C. Answer choice B only concerns certain customers, whereas answer choice C indicates more generally that a cost/benefit analysis should be made. Answer choice D is incorrect because, like answer choice B, it only concerns a certain subset of book defects. Answer choice E is incorrect because, like the conclusion in the question, it ignores whether additional costs will be outweighed by additional benefits. It simply indicates that additional investment will bring additional benefits.

11. Answer choice D is correct because it best articulates the conclusion that noises may or may not be indications of danger. Answer choice A is incorrect because a car can have squeaks and rattling and still be safe under the facts of the question. Answer choice B is incorrect because the facts of the question indicate only that cars on rough roads can have squeaks and rattling. Answer choice C is incorrect because it is okay to have a noise that is not an indication of danger. People do not necessarily have to perform maintenance to avoid such noises. Answer choice E is incorrect because it is not a conclusion that flows directly from the statements in the question. While it may be a conclusion that is generally true, it is not as direct a conclusion from the facts of the question as is the conclusion for answer choice D.

12. Answer choice A is correct because the student concludes the island is a good vacation place based on the opinion of the friends. Answer choice B is incorrect because the island can be a good vacation place even if some things distract from that fact. Answer choice C is incorrect because it is not necessary to be on vacation to form an opinion about whether a place is a good vacation spot. Answer choice D is incorrect because the beliefs of most people are not necessarily correct with respect to whether the island is a good vacation place. Answer choice E is incorrect because a busy airport and harbor do not contribute to making a place a good vacation spot.

13. Answer choice C is correct because it most clearly establishes a reason, other than racial discrimination, for the educational level of African immigrants. Answer choice A gives an explanation for the difference in education levels, but is not as strong as answer choice C. Answer choice C, in using white immigrants as a reference point, most strongly contradicts the conclusion of racial discrimination. Answer choice A makes no

such comparison, and is thus not as strong. Answer choice B is incorrect because a comparison to a different people group does not change the status of African immigrants relative to the American population under the facts of the question. Answer choice D is incorrect because it does not explain why African immigrants in particular do not have as many advanced degrees as the American population. Answer choice E is wrong because it is not on point.

14. Answer choice B is correct because it articulates the conclusion that something other than eating habits is responsible for the presence of cancer in elderly people. Answer choice A is incorrect because it does not address a shortcoming in the study that the researcher critiques. Answer choice C is incorrect because it is inaccurate. The researcher does not believe the conclusion that he or she arrives at is obvious. Answer choice D is incorrect because it is focused on what the reader should do, and not on the shortcomings of the study critiqued by the researcher. Answer choice E is incorrect because it is too extreme. A healthy diet can have the consequence that you will live longer, and by living longer there is a higher likelihood of suffering from the adverse consequence of cancer.

15. Answer choice D is correct because the facts in the question indicate that it is not possible to be a good leader without having followed a good leader. The facts of the question set up the following chain of reasoning: to be a good leader you must have been a good follower; to be a good follower you must have had a good leader; therefore, to be a good leader you must have been a good follower of another good leader.

Answer choice A is incorrect because the question does not concern itself with the difficulty of finding a leader. Answer choice B is incorrect because the question deals with who teaches good leadership and who acquires such leadership. The question does not deal with the issue of whether the leadership is acquired through experience or natural ability. Answer choice C is incorrect because it concerns a specific aspect of leadership, not with how leadership skills are taught and learned in general. Answer choice E is incorrect because it concerns *effective* leadership, and not *good* leadership in particular. It could be a correct response; however, answer choice D is better because it specifically concerns good leadership.

16. Answer choice A is correct because it is not clear from the facts that cooperation will necessarily be possible. The fact that there is currently an increased understanding of herbal extracts does not by itself mean that cooperation between modern medicine and alternative medicine practitioners will certainly follow. Answer choice B is incorrect because it articulates the inverse of what the question articulates. A lack of understanding about an issue does not prove that attaining an understanding about the issue will ensure cooperation. Answer choice C is incorrect because the significance of herbal extracts to alternative medicine does not directly affect the ability of alternative medicine practitioners to cooperate with others on issues relating to herbal extracts. Answer choice D is incorrect because, while discovery and acceptance of herbal extract cures in the future may help cooperation, they do not establish that cooperation in the present will be achieved. Answer choice E is incorrect because cooperation is possible, regardless of whether the herbal extracts are in fact effective.

17. A is incorrect because Lani does not indicate Chacho is correct. B is incorrect because Lani questions Chacho's conclusion, not the survey. C is correct. Chacho's conclusion is less strong with the information offered by Lani. D is incorrect because Chacho's method of argument is not questioned by Lani. She offers new information. E could be correct, but it is not the best answer because it is too harsh on Chacho. Lani questions his conclusion, but does not argue it is incorrect.

18. Answer choice B is correct because the facts of the question indicate that labor costs were one of the factors that made goods cheaper. The other factors that made goods cheaper may have been responsible for keeping the country out of recession. Answer choice A is incorrect because the passage concerns the growth of the economy, not social justice with respect to poor working people. Answer choice C is incorrect because it does not establish why, under the specific facts provided in the question, the argument can be called into question. Answer choice C may be a true statement, but it is not as good an answer as choice B. Answer choice D is incorrect because it is a critique of economists in general, and not of the reasoning in this particular question. Answer choice E is incorrect because, like answer choice C, it is a more general statement about economic analysis.

19. Answer choice A is correct because it articulates how users have been able to go from just playing games with computers to using them for small business tasks as well. Answer choice B is incorrect because the passage does not indicate what will happen in the future. It merely discusses the trajectory the computer industry has followed so far. Answer choice C is incorrect because the passage does not discuss a lag between the existence of computing power and a point in time when such computing power is put to use. Answer choice D is incorrect because, as is indicated with respect to answer choice B above, the passage does not discuss the future. Answer choice E is incorrect because the passage does not discuss what users should do with their computers. It simply discusses what they have done in the past.

20. Answer choice E is correct because the facts of the question indicate that company beverages can only be made by following the original recipe. Answer choice A is incorrect because it is possible under the facts of the question that many additional beverages remain to be discovered. Answer choice B is incorrect because it is consistent with the facts in the question. Companies with valuable recipes will probably take steps to protect those recipes. Answer choice C is incorrect because the passage does not preclude the possibility that valuable recipes were discovered by accident. Answer choice D is incorrect because the passage does not preclude the possibility that beverage makeup may be studied by other people. The passage does say however, that an exact recipe must be followed to reproduce the qualities of a beverage.

21. Answer choice A is correct because, under the facts of the question, gambling has good and bad consequences. To arrive at the conclusion that gambling should be promoted, one must believe that the good consequences outweigh the bad. Answer choice press B is incorrect because it is not as strong as answer choice A. Answer choice

B compares one good aspect of gambling to one bad aspect. Answer choice A takes a broader view of the issue by focusing on improving the "life of citizens". This is also what the facts of the question focus on. Answer choice C is incorrect because the overall wellness of citizens can be improved, even if economic conditions in certain cities deteriorate. Answer choice D is incorrect because the analysis does not depend on what people want to do. Answer choice E is incorrect because the passage does not compare gambling to other forms of economic activity.

22. A is incorrect because all the positive information presented is from a source that has a reason to present positive information. B is correct. This is a conclusion one could draw from the facts, but it does not establish a reason to question the commercial. C is incorrect because the study results concern only limited factors that go into a determination of whether one truck is better than another. D and E are both incorrect. These valid factors for what constitutes a better truck were not referenced in the commercial.

23. Answer choice C is correct because people must want the outcome promised by the advertisement for the advertisement to be effective. Answer choice A is incorrect because an advertisement can be effective even if the studies that it is based on are not accurate. Answer choice B is incorrect because the existence of alternatives does not establish that this particular method will not be sold through an advertisement. Answer choice D is incorrect because readers could give the product a try, even if they do not trust the advertisement. Answer choice E is incorrect because, regardless of whether having a young appearance is a good thing, the advertisement will be effective if its audience wants to appear younger.

24. Answer choice A is correct because the author draws a conclusion about the likelihood of a storm from the level of seashells. Answer choice B is incorrect because the author does not arrive at a conclusion about when storms will not assail the point. Answer choice C is incorrect because it misstates the reasoning in the question. The question reasons that seashell levels are an indicator of storms, but do not themselves cause storms. Answer choice D is incorrect because the author does not detect a change in weather patterns. Instead, the question assumes that past weather patterns will continue. Answer choice E is incorrect because it is not as strong as answer choice A. Under the facts of the question, it appears the author believes that storms come through at specific intervals. Over time, seashells are eroded away. Thus, a low level of seashells would signal that the end of the interval between storms is approaching. If tourists, and not currents, suddenly lowered the level of seashells, then the above reasoning would not hold. However, tourists can also remove seashells at an even pace, like currents could, and thus answer choice E is not a necessary assumption.

25. Answer choice B is correct because it explains how Rob won the race without maintaining a high level of speed. With all the other contestants out of the race, Rob did not have to go fast to win the race. Answer choices A and D are wrong because they tend to contradict, rather than explain, the outcome in the facts of the question. While the question indicates that cars must stop to refuel at least three times, answer choices A and

D imply that Rob did not stop at least three times. Answer choices C and D are incorrect because answer choice B is stronger. Rob is more likely to win a race in which all the other contestants have been animated, than he is to win a race in which all other contestants remain active participants. These answer choices are close though, making this a tough question.

26. Answer choice C is correct because it articulates why a liberal arts education is desirable under the facts of the question. Answer choice A is incorrect because what some successful people have in terms of education is not necessarily applicable to everyone. Answer choice B is incorrect because it is not as strong as answer choice C. Answer choice B basically indicates that a liberal arts education is more desirable because it is more interesting. However, answer choice C identifies the versatility (which will allow workers to deal with changing technological and economic conditions mentioned in the question) that will give workers a substantial increase in well-being. Answer choice D is incorrect because, while it may be true, outsourcing is not a factor that is specifically mentioned in the question. Answer choice E is incorrect because it does not address the merits of the education. Students selecting a liberal arts education may have had a higher IQ than other students.

SECTION II: READING COMPREHENSION

1. Response A could be correct, but it is not the best response. From the passage it appears that the game influenced society, and caused casualties through social unrest. However, there is no indication that there was a large amount of social unrest, and therefore the author would not necessarily believe that a lot of people died. Among the athletes, only the captain of the losing team would get killed. The author does not indicate how often the games were played, therefore it is difficult to arrive at a conclusion about how many people died because of this game.

Response B is not correct because there is no information in the passage to support it. While the Spanish destroyed historical records, there is no indication that they advocated a form of entertainment that involves the death of people. Thus, it is possible to conclude that the Spanish were *less* violent than the Toltecs. While it is a historical fact that the Spanish also killed people, that information is not found in the passage.

Response C could be correct, but there is no indication in the passage that it is in fact correct. It appears from the passage that the decline of the Mayan civilization coincided with the fact that the game ceased to be played. However, there is no indication that one of those events caused the other.

There is simply no information in the passage to indicate whether one group of people was better at the game than other people. Thus, answer D is not correct.

Answer E is correct. The author does not seem to condemn the fact that the captains themselves could get killed. In fact, the author implies that their death may have been an act of justice because those athletes enabled a brutal sport. However, the suffering caused in the society because of the games is something that the author clearly believes was wrong. This is accentuated by the sentence "Their blood rests on the hands of the athletes..."

2.   Response A could be correct, but it is not the best answer. The author believes that the game was not just. Nonetheless, that view is tempered by the author's recognition that it is difficult to arrive at conclusions about the game because of the incomplete historical record. Therefore, response B is correct. The passage discusses what appears to have been a violent game, and then qualifies that discussion with information about the accuracy of the historical record that calls into question the conclusions about the game.

Answer C is incorrect because the passage does not present a variety of alternative conclusions about the past and does not express an inability to choose between such conclusions. Rather, the passage contains one set of specific conclusions that are qualified by the lack of a complete historical record.

Answer D is incorrect because the passage does not discuss the oppressed. It discusses the victims of the violence caused by the game. While oppressed people can be thought of as victims, here it is not clear that the victims of the violence were part of an oppressed group of people. It is possible that a wealthy ruler, not an oppressed person, would get killed by violence resulting from the game.

Answer E is incorrect because the passage says nothing about the future.

3.   Answer choice A is incorrect because there is no indication in the passage of the game's effectiveness in defusing social tension relative to other means of defusing such tension.

Answer choice B is a possible conclusion, but it is not the best response. The passage indicates that the Toltecs "arrived" and that their "influence appeared" in the Mayan culture. While their arrival and influence may have been the result of a conquest, it may have also been the result of trade, or other peaceful means of influence.

Answer choice C is also a permissible conclusion. The fact that athletes participated in this violent game voluntarily, with the possibility of acquiring fame, indicates that the game may have been entertaining. However, this is not the best response.

Choice D is the best response because the game appears to have caused social unrest and innocent deaths when its rules were changed. Those two adverse outcomes are clearly stated in the passage and thus this conclusion flows most directly from the passage.

Choice E is incorrect because there is no information in the passage that indicates the level of fairness of most games. While the passage indicates that the consequences of a wrong call by a referee could be disastrous, there is no indication as to how often that occurred, if at all.

4.   Answer choice A is correct. The author arrives at some strong conclusions about the game's victims. The information about the Spanish tempers those strong conclusions. Answer choice B is incorrect because nobody is blamed for the decline of the game. If anything, the decline of the game was a good thing.

Answer choice C is incorrect because no information is provided as to why the civilization declined. Choice D is incorrect. The information about the Spanish is part of an explanation as to why our current knowledge of the game is limited. The passage does not explain how historical research has, or will, change the fact that our knowledge about the game is limited.

Answer choice E is incorrect because no solution to the incomplete historical record appears in the passage. The Spanish helped cause the fact that we have an incomplete historical record. From the passage, there does not appear to be a way to reverse that loss.

5.   Answer choice A is wrong because the passage says nothing about peoples of the present. Answer choice B is correct. The passage endorses the game as it existed before the rules were changed to make it deadly. Also, this answer choice makes a general conclusion about "defusing social tension." This general conclusion is consistent with the passage's statement that it is difficult to arrive at more precise conclusions about the game because of the incomplete historical record.

Choice C is incorrect because the use of the word "always" in the answer is too extreme. In fact, the passage sees nothing wrong with the game insofar as it kills people who enable the game's existence.

Answer choice D is also too extreme. The passage indicates that it is not possible to come to definite conclusions, but this does not foreclose the possibility of learning lessons from what we do know about the game. Answer choice E is consistent with the passage, but is not the most consistent. The passage speaks highly of modern sports, saying that they diffuse tension. This does not foreclose the possibility that modern sports may have some problems, including problems of the Maya game. However, there is no discussion in the passage about any issues that modern sports face. Thus, answer choice B is more consistent with this passage than is answer choice E.

6.   This passage may cause you to feel strong emotions because of the opinions expressed in it about matters that can be controversial. To correctly answer the questions, you need to keep your emotions in check and be sensitive to exactly what this passage is saying.

Answer choice A is wrong because the author wants to increase the welfare of all humanity, which includes the poor. Answer choice B is wrong because the author does not call into question the trustworthiness of the poor, nor does the author indicate that people are poor because of their lack of trustworthiness. In fact, the author indicates in the second paragraph that inequality arises because of different abilities.

Answer choice C is wrong because the author does not indicate that the poor should be helped simply because they are poor. Rather, the author appears to be focused on generating wealth for everyone, regardless of whether they are already wealthy or poor. Answer choice D is wrong because the author is not judgmental towards the poor. The author attributes property to differing levels of abilities, which is a view that does not necessarily reflect badly on poor people.

Answer choice E is correct because the author, though analyzing the poor within the context of wealth allocation in society, does not advocate for the poor nor does the author identify with them.

7.   Answer choice A is wrong because it is specifically contradicted in the passage. The passage indicates that wealthy people can actually have a higher level of well-being by reducing their wealth.

Answer choice B is correct. The author indicates that there are disadvantages to having too much and too little inequality, and also indicates that it is extremely difficult to set the exact level of inequality that is most beneficial. The solution is to have a level of inequality that exists within a certain range.

Answer choice C is wrong because, while it is an accurate statement of what the passage indicates, it is not the main point of the passage. The author is focused on establishing an appropriate level of inequality, and mentions the distortions in the media as being a factor that complicates this task.

Answer choice D is wrong because it overstates the difficulties that the author sees with regard to policies that govern inequality. While the passage acknowledges that it is difficult to determine an appropriate level of inequality, it suggests a strategy for dealing with such difficulty.

Answer choice E is wrong because the passage does not focus on how people's efforts create wealth. Rather, it focuses on how wealth allocation can maximize wealth by influencing how existing wealth is put to use. Under the thinking of the passage, poor people, if they have less abilities than a wealthy person, may not create more wealth than the wealthy person even if they exert a higher level of effort. If such wealthy person can create more wealth than the poor person, the author reasons that the wealthy person should have more wealth, regardless of that person's level of effort.

8.   Answer choice A is not the best answer because the author would not necessarily agree with the answer. Because of the author's focus on maximizing wealth creation, the author may agree to give more money to the rich if that will maximize wealth creation, even if the rich also purchase a yacht with their wealth.

Answer choice B is not the best answer because it does not touch on the author's focus on wealth creation. If other sectors of society will also misspend the wealth, then the author would not advocate taking it away from the poor. This answer choice is something the author could agree to under the right circumstances. However, this is not the best answer because a redistribution plan that follows this answer choice would not necessarily create wealth.

Answer choice C is correct because it articulates an informed and proven way to generate wealth.

Answer choice D is incorrect for the same reasons that answer choice B is incorrect. This kind of redistribution plan will not necessarily generate more wealth because other sectors of the population may also misspend it.

Answer choice E is clearly wrong because the passage is about how to go about redistributing wealth.

9.   Answer choice A is wrong because it is too strong a statement. While the author indicates that inequality can do good things, the author also indicates that inequality has bad consequences. Thus, inequality is, by itself, neither good nor bad. Rather, the level of inequality is what matters under the analysis of the passage.

Answer choice B is wrong because, while difficult to do, the passage indicates that rebalancing may have to occur if inequality reaches a level that is not optimal.

Answer choice C is correct because the passage indicates that wealthy people may benefit by having less wealth. Answer choice D is incorrect because it takes the passage's statement about vacations and uses it out of context. The passage does not say that vacations are a bad thing. Rather, it indicates that increasing the number of vacations for the middle class has is not necessarily a good thing.

Answer choice E is incorrect because it is too strong. The passage indicates that the media distorts the inequality issue in order to attract readership. The sensationalism is a product of that effort, and not the product of a conscious misinformation effort.

10. Answer choice A is wrong because it does not reflect the author's reasoning. The author's picture of inequality may be distorted, but that is not the reason why the author lists the benefits of any quality. Answer choice B is wrong for the same reason. While the author may in fact offend some readers, that is not the author's purpose for including the information.

Answer choice C is incorrect because, while the information may in fact call into question commonly held beliefs, that is not the precise reason for why the author lists the information. As answer choice D indicates, the author lists the benefits of inequality to lend support to the author's conclusion that a certain amount of inequality should exist. Thus, answer choice D more clearly articulates the author's reason for including the information.

Like answer choices A and B, answer choice E may in fact be correct, but it does not reflect the reason for why the author included the information about the benefits of inequality.

11. Answer choice A is correct. These kinds of skilled people will receive more wealth under the views expressed in the passage. Whether they actually use the wealth to create more wealth is not entirely certain. That is why, as the passage indicates, making a decision about inequality is difficult.

Answer choice B is incorrect because people who exert much effort to generate wealth will not necessarily benefit under the views expressed in the passage. The passage is focused on the actual generation of wealth, not the level of effort put into generating wealth.

Answer choice C is incorrect because an increase in wealth for all humanity will not necessarily benefit the poor. The passage does not contain a mechanism for allocating wealth to the poor to meet their needs. While it is possible that an overall increase in wealth will benefit the poor the most, answer choice A is better because the people identified in the choice will directly obtain wealth under the policies articulated in this passage.

Answer choice D is incorrect because it is not the best answer. While the middle-class could benefit by following the views of the passage, they will not directly obtain wealth. Also, the passage does not identify with any specificity what the middle-class should spend its money on.

Answer choice E is incorrect because, under certain circumstances, the passage indicates that the wealthy should have wealth taken away from them.

12. Answer choice A is wrong because it is inconsistent with the passage. The passage indicates that skilled people can generate wealth in a variety of different ways.

Answer choice B is correct. The passage does not define exactly what level of inequality is appropriate. Rather, it lists a variety of considerations to be taken into account to determine how wealth should be distributed.

While the author does criticize the media, that is not the main purpose of the passage. Instead, the passage is about how to allocate wealth, and the media is listed as something that stands in the way of that task. Answer choice C is thus incorrect.

Answer choice D is incorrect because, while it might be true, it is not the main purpose of the passage. The purpose of the passage is to increase total wealth. It is not to increase wealth for a particular group of people.

The passage does not contain a formula for wealth allocation. Indeed, the passage implies that it is not possible to have a formula because of the difficulty of making decisions about wealth allocation. Answer choice E is thus incorrect.

13. This passage may elicit strong emotions from some of its readers. You may find yourself agreeing, or strongly disagreeing, with what the author says. To maximize the points you receive on the exam you must not let yourself be influenced by such feelings during the exam. You must focus on exactly what the passage says, and what the questions ask. This passage does not reflect my views, so please do not send me letters protesting its content. If you feel compelled to send me a letter concerning this passage, please do so after you take the actual LSAT.

Here, answer choice C is correct. The author does not have a high opinion of men because they are called "oppressors." The author uncritically presents Dr. Casper's attack on "progress" that some people believe has occurred. The attack on such "progress" implies that women are currently no better off than they have been in the past. Thus, the author would likely agree with a statement that men have distorted the past and the notion of equality to convince women that they have progressed from the past to a more equal position in society.

Answer choice A is wrong because the author believes all women in certain professions (not just "deserving women") are not fairly compensated. Answer choice B is wrong because the passage is not concerned with the welfare of humanity. Its focus is on women. In addition, the author notes that women themselves are often the perpetrators of injustice against them.

Answer choice D is wrong because the passage implies that men are likely somewhat conscious participants in what the author believes is unequal treatment of women. Answer choice E is wrong because it does not concern specifically the welfare of women, and the author implies that it is not possible to have guidance with respect to the oppression discussed in the passage.

14. Answer choice A is correct because the passage speaks of gender differences as being something that are not understood, even by women themselves. Answer choice B is wrong because it is not accurate. The passage indicates that, while men are better off, women are not. It is possible that social welfare has increased in general, but welfare for women, according to the passage, has not. Answer choice C is wrong because the passage indicates that men are not necessarily consciously engaging in a process that has created the current conditions of women. Answer choice D is wrong because the passage indicates that women do not in fact engage in activities, such as professional careers, in

the same way that men do. Answer choice E is wrong because the passage indicates women do not in fact have more wealth. While their earnings have increased, so have the demands on them.

15. Answer choice E is correct because it most closely articulates the issue that most sociologists have with Dr. Casper. Without giving things numerical values, it is difficult to compare them with precision. Answer choice A is wrong because it is too strong a statement. If Dr. Casper developed a method for assigning numerical values to "sacrifices", that would address the issue that most sociologists have with her research. Answer choice B is wrong because the entire view of "most sociologists" is not given in the passage. Rather, the passage gives one issue that most sociologists have with Dr. Casper's research. Answer choice C is wrong because an alternative approach is not given. The passage simply mentions a shortcoming that most sociologists see in Dr. Casper's findings. Answer choice D is correct, but answer choice E is a better answer because it is more closely tied into the facts of this passage.

16. Answer choice D is correct, not because its statements are in fact true, but because it correctly articulates what the author set out to do. Answer choice A is wrong because, among other things, the passage is not critical of an approach that does not follow analytical steps for modern scientific inquiry. Answer choice B is wrong because the passage does not explore alternative avenues. Answer choice C is wrong because it is too broad. The author challenges understandings of women's roles, not our understanding of the world. Answer choice E is wrong because, while it accurately describes what the passage does, it does not describe the passage's main purpose.

17. Answer choice B is correct because in the second paragraph the author seeks to establish how "progress" on women's issues has had adverse consequences. Answer choice A is wrong because the author gives the medical profession as an example of a wider reality. The author does not single out the medical profession as being a profession that is particularly bad in terms of how it treats women. Answer choice C is wrong because the acts of men are not necessarily conscious according to the passage. Thus, they would not necessarily be able to enter into a conspiracy. Answer choice D is incorrect because, while it articulates something that the author would probably agree with, it is not what the author seeks to accomplish. The author speaks of women in general, not about particular problems in particular professions. Answer choice E is wrong because a solution is not readily apparent from the passage.

18. Answer choice A is correct because Dr. Casper seems to have an almost fatalistic approach to the condition of women. Answer choice B is incorrect because there is nothing in the passage that indicates that Dr. Casper disagrees with the critique of most sociologists with respect to articulating her findings in numerical terms. It is possible that Dr. Casper has not articulated her findings numerically because it has not been a priority for her. Answer choice C is wrong because Dr. Casper approaches well-being as a zero sum game. For example, she believes one reason that men are better off is because women are not necessarily better off. Answer choice D is wrong because Dr. Casper believes the issue is more complex. She points out that, even though women now occupy

positions of leadership in our society, they are not necessarily better off. Answer choice E is wrong because Dr. Casper probably does not believe that women fail to take responsibility for their actions. While Dr. Casper believes women harm themselves, Dr. Casper probably believes it is because they are misguided.

19. Answer choice C is correct. While women do more tasks with rewards than in the past, they also have more demands placed on them. According to the passage, those demands are greater than they should be. Answer choice A is incorrect because the passage clearly implicates men, and not just women, for the troubled relationship it describes. Answer choice B is incorrect because it is too extreme. While the passage does have some fatalistic hints, it does not foreclose the possibility that a solution can be found. Answer choice D is incorrect because the passage in fact seeks to unravel some of the complexities of the relationship between men and women. Answer choice E is incorrect because the author clearly indicates that advances have not necessarily helped women.

20. Answer choice B is correct because, while the author understands the benefits of the proposed legislation, the author also sees the benefits of the existing legal framework. Answer choice A is incorrect. The passage discusses how the area could be even more productive. The passage does not seek to reverse a situation in which the land has become less productive. Answer choice C is incorrect because the passage does not provide information from which to infer the competence of nonfarmer voters. Answer choice D is incorrect because creating subdivisions and enabling wildlife are more than marginally beneficial. Answer choice E is incorrect because the author has simply presented the findings of Clear Blue University, but does not express agreement with them.

21. Answer choice E is correct because the exact provisions of legislation ordinarily cannot be used for a purpose that is contrary to the purpose of the legislation. Answer choice A is incorrect because a known potential consequence of the legislation is that land values will decline if water rights are separated from the land. Answer choice B is incorrect because it is not as strong as answer choice E. The fact that an activity is harmful, by itself, does not necessarily make it illegal. Answer choice C is incorrect because the legislation was not explicitly worded to provide for developer profitability. Answer choice D is incorrect because, as with answer choice B, the fact that something is harmful does not necessarily make it illegal.

22. Answer choice E is correct because the passage does not support one constituency over another in its discussion of water rights. Answer choice A is incorrect because the use of the river is at the center of the discussion about the economic activity surrounding the river. Answer choice B is incorrect because it is consistent with the findings of the University study. Answer choice C is incorrect because the possibility that the water is not as pure as it should be is what gives rise to the debate about how to use the water. Answer choice D is incorrect because one can conclude from the passage that the economic activity surrounding the river would be greater if the legal structure governing water rights were changed.

23. Answer choice D is correct because the proposed legislation would leave water rights in the hands of farmers, but would place the farming industry in a more precarious position long term. Answer choice A is incorrect because it is possible that certain Greene Citizens are also farmers. Answer choice B is incorrect because it is possible that the citizen group is aware of the complexity of the issues, such as those identified by the University study. Answer choice C is incorrect because the Green Citizens seek to advance the welfare of wildlife, and not their own specific welfare. Answer choice E is incorrect because the proposed legislation could actually increase development.

24. Answer choice A is correct because the University study establishes that the proposed legislation may not be necessary. Answer choice B is incorrect because there is no indication that the developers are consciously supporting the legislation for a wrong reason. Answer choice C is incorrect because the author does not attack the reasoning of the Citizens. Rather, the author simply indicates that, with the University study, the same outcome can be achieved with the existing framework. Answer choice D is incorrect because the University study affirms the existing legal framework and does not propose a new one. Answer choice E is incorrect because the outcome of the legislation, not the assumptions about it, is what the University study calls into question.

25. Answer choice C is correct because the other answer choices are all wrong. While the author discusses the positions that certain groups of people have taken with respect to the legislation, the author does not articulate a view with respect to the people who will vote on the legislation. The author does not advocate the passage of the legislation, and instead gives the pros and cons of it.

26. Answer choice B is correct because, if the legislation is passed, it will be more profitable to build homes along the river. Answer choice A is wrong because no mention is made of any kind of crop grown along the river. Answer choice C is incorrect because the passage does not indicate whether the critique of the University study is the final word on whether the legislation is useful. Answer choice D is incorrect because, while it appears that some farmers may agree with the Green Citizens, we do not know whether some farmers are in fact members of that group. Answer choice E is incorrect because no information in this respect is given in the passage. We do not know the current water level, what the water level would be with the legislation, or what the water level should be.

SECTION III: LOGICAL REASONING

1. A is correct. The trees will not, by themselves, develop the desolate lot. This is Peter's point. B is correct, but it is not Peter's point. He implies other lots may not require as much care, but he is primarily concerned with what to do with *this* lot. C is a general statement that does not apply to Peter. He says nothing about whether the proper approach is readily evident. D is incorrect because Peter does not plot alternatives. He suggests one approach. E is incorrect because Peter does not refer to a counterproductive solution.

2.   Answer choice C is correct because it establishes how a disconnect exists between annual income and the standard of living. Answer choice A is incorrect because it does not explain how those advances benefit the residents while their income falls. Answer choice B is incorrect because a decline in residents does not by itself explain the rise in the standard of living. Answer choice D is incorrect because a bigger decline in annual income elsewhere also does not explain how the standard of living rose in Bigville. Answer choice E is incorrect because answer choice C is a stronger answer. Answer choice E does not indicate whether methods for calculating the standard of living changed during the 10 year period in question, or whether the discrepancy was caused because two different methods that were used. Answer choice C provides a more direct explanation for the discrepancy.

3.   Answer choice E is correct because Hinterton Valley sparkling wines can be cheaper than some Cantor Valley white wines. With respect to the sparkling wines, we do not know exactly how they are priced in one valley compared to the other. We just know that they are the cheapest wines in their respective valleys. Because most Hinterton Valley white wines are more expensive than Cantor Valley white wines, we know that a Hinterton Valley sparkling wine can be cheaper than some Cantor Valley wines and also be cheaper than all Hinterton Valley white wines. Answer choice A is wrong because the cheapest Cantor Valley sparkling wine would have to be cheaper than *all* Cantor Valley wines (not just some of them). Answer choice B is incorrect because all red Hinterton Valley wines must be more expensive than all the cheaper Cantor Valley wines. Answer choice C is a possible solution. However, answer choice E is stronger because sparkling wines are cheaper than white wines. Answer choice D is incorrect because a red Cantor Valley wine cannot be cheaper than a white wine from the same Valley.

4.   Answer choice A is correct because it links the homeowners in the survey and the voting public. For the survey's conclusion to be valid, the homeowners that were surveyed must also be voters who influence legislation. Answer choice B is incorrect because the views of all homeowners will not necessarily affect the popularity of legislation if the homeowners are not also voters. Answer choice C is incorrect because it does not articulate an assumption; it simply gives additional facts. Answer choice D, while correct, is too broad. Answer choice A is correct because it applies more specifically to this fact pattern. Answer choice E is incorrect because it does not concern the specific factual situation presented in this question, namely that a piece of legislation will not pass because it was identified as unpopular in a survey.

5.   Answer choice D is correct because it restates the conclusion that it is better to have things that last longer. That way, you do not have to go through the transition that occurs when something wears out or dies. Answer choice A is wrong because it does not address the circumstance in which a transition occurs because of a shorter life span. Answer choice B is wrong because its logical structure is different. Making a selfish decision is different from making a decision to more closely align your lifespan with that of something else to avoid grief. Answer choice C is wrong because, while it is

consistent with the reasoning in the question, it does not parallel the argument structure in the question. Answer choice E is incorrect because answer choice D is a better answer. Even elderly humans can out-live dogs, and this would be especially true if an elderly human owned an elderly dog.

6. Answer choice B is correct because it articulates the belief that you should support organizations that only engage in activities that you believe in. In other words, you should not participate in an organization if the organization does anything you disagree with. Answer choice A is incorrect because it does not support the critic's actual position. It could be a conclusion that you arrive at because of the critic's position. Namely, if it is not good to invest in the oil tankers because they hurt animals, maybe one should do something to help the animals. Answer choice C is incorrect because it seeks to justify a position that is the opposite of the critic's position. Answer choices D and E are incorrect because, like answer choice A, they could be conclusions that you arrive at because of the critic's argument. However, they do not themselves support the argument.

7. A is incorrect because its distinction is not germane to this question. B is incorrect because no spatial relationship exists in this question. C may look tempting. The author concludes that a certain approach is the proper one for a specific reason. The author does not make an assumption about another approach. Thus, C is incorrect. D is incorrect because the conclusion does not establish a causal connection. E is correct. The author concludes that *no* X Co. bearings should be used because *certain* of them are flawed.

8. Answer choice A is correct because the question attributes the good bug situation to the act of Mr. Rodriguez; even though from the facts of the question, it is not entirely clear that he had, in fact, caused the good bug situation. Answer choice B is incorrect because, whether or not Mr. Rodriguez has similar crops, the question concludes that there are fewer bugs on his farm because of his actions (not because of the kind of crop he grows or doesn't grow). Answer choice C is incorrect because it is not a necessary assumption. As with the kind of crop grown (discussed in answer choice B above), the nature of the land is not necessary to the conclusion that Mr. Rodriguez was the reason why there were fewer bugs on his farm. Answer choice D is incorrect because it does not address the link between Mr. Rodriguez's actions and the lower bug population. Answer choice E is incorrect because the question does not state that Mr. Rodriguez used pesticides, and the lower bug population can be the result of something other than the use of pesticides.

9. Answer choice A is correct because inhospitable crops would explain the decline in bug population. Answer choice B is clearly wrong because bug population does not depend on whether a farmer is a good person. Answer choice C is wrong because it does not describe what might be the cause of the lower bug population. The effect of a lower bug population may be higher crop yield, but that does not explain why the bug population is lower to begin with. Answer choice D is wrong because, like answer choice B, having something good does not mean that bugs will not populate a particular farm. Answer choice E is wrong because it is not linked to the specific facts of this

question. Neither the question, nor answer choice E itself, indicates whether genetically engineered crops are being used.

10. Answer choice D is correct because it proves that people intuitively knew the truth, and did not infer the truth from any inflection in the speaker's voice. Answer choice A is incorrect because smart older experienced people may have acquired a knowledge of the truth through their intelligence, age, and experience. Such knowledge of the truth would not be intuitive for all humans. Answer choice B is incorrect because an inability to discern a half-truth does not prove a person's ability to discern the truth. Answer choice C is incorrect because answer choice D is stronger. In answer choice D the study was performed on humans. Answer choice E is incorrect because the question concerns whether humans have an intuitive sense of the truth, not what effect truth has on them.

11. Answer choice B is correct because a substantial increase in gas, which is part of a substantial portion of the budget, would help explain the 10 percent increase in a manner inconsistent with the utility's justification. Answer choice A is incorrect because what most utilities do does not directly explain what this particular utility is doing. Answer choice C is incorrect because it does not attack the utility's justification. The utility says it is increasing expenditures on things such as solar energy, which it could do even if it were not cost-effective to do so. Answer choice D is incorrect because, while it provides a basis for attacking the credibility of the utility, it does not directly contradict the utility in the manner that answer choice B does. Answer choice E is incorrect because, while an increase in the CEO's salary provides some explanation as to why the utility would want to shift the explanation for rate increases to other things, it is not as strong an explanation as answer B.

12. E is correct because, as students' access to information changes, their level of ability and potential for accomplishment also changes. Answers A and B are incorrect because they plainly do not explain the conflict. Answer C is wrong because, while the Principal's statements suffer from the shortcomings described in this answer choice, those shortcomings are not the best explanation for the conflict. Answer choice D is wrong because, like answer choice C, the shortcomings described are not the best explanation for the conflict.

13. Answer choice A is correct because it attacks the argument's standard for what a "worthy cause" is. If the worthiness of the project depends on its popularity (not necessarily its usefulness) then the project in question is worthy if it is popular. Answer choice B is incorrect because it does not indicate why this particular statue is a worthy cause. Answer choice C is incorrect because the merits of the golden statue are at issue. The nature of the single biggest issue facing the community is not at issue in this question. Answer choice D is incorrect because the affordability of taxes is not at issue in this question. Answer choice E is incorrect because it is not as good as answer choice A. The statue is not useful, even if Mr. Jones is a good person. Thus, this answer choice does not attack the basic standard found in the fact of the question, namely that something useless is not a worthy cause.

14. Answer choice E is correct because it explains why participation in Native American activities did not increase, even though enrollment of people claiming to be Native American increased substantially. Answer choice A is incorrect because it presents additional information, and not a conclusion that can be drawn from the facts in the question. Answer choice B is incorrect because it does not address the discrepancy identified in the question. Regardless of whether the definition of "Native American" is not clear, why did participation in Native American activities not increase when the number of people identifying themselves as Native Americans increased substantially? Answer choice C is incorrect because it is not as strong as answer E. Answer choice C concludes that the people identifying themselves as Native Americans were not in fact Native Americans. Answer choice E allows for the conclusion that such people are simply not commonly thought of as being Native Americans. They may have had an ancestor who was Native American, but they themselves are not active in Native American matters. Answer choice D is incorrect because it is not a conclusion that can be drawn from the facts of the question. The facts do not indicate whether other groups were or were not funded.

15. Answer choice C is correct because Bob creates more pollution after having used the government program than he would otherwise. Answer choice A is incorrect because it is too broad. It is possible that, on balance, the program benefits the environment. Answer choice B is incorrect because it is not as good as answer choice C. The solution proposed in answer choice B is not entirely practical because figuring out what people are thinking is very difficult to do with a government program. Thus, it is not clear from the facts that the program must be changed (especially considering that it is possible that the program substantially benefits the environment). Answer choice D is incorrect because, as is indicated above, it is possible that the program on balance reduces pollution. Answer choice E is incorrect because Bob has not breached any provision of the program. Thus, he should not be penalized.

16. A is correct. Margret broadens the criteria from last year's accident to argue that the speed limit has value. B is incorrect because Margret does not discuss last year's accident. C is incorrect because Margret does not establish how the speed limit should be set. D is incorrect because Margret does not point out an assumption made by John. E could be correct. A is better though, because it more closely describes Margret's argument. John's blanket conclusion, "obeying the speed limit is of no value," applies to actual and potential usefulness. If John had considered that distinction he may have changed his conclusion.

17. Answer choice A is correct because it not only highlights the importance of a person's ability to do a task, it discounts people's preferences. Thus, it articulates what the question does not overtly state, namely that people's preference for tall people is not justified. Answer choice B is incorrect because it does not articulate the core assumptions of the question as well as answer choice A. Answer choice B indicates that other things should be given "more weight," but does not indicate that aesthetic preferences (such as height) should be discounted. Answer choice C is wrong because

the passage does not compare abilities of tall and short people. Rather, it concerns the criteria that people use when evaluating short versus tall people. Answer choices D and E are wrong because the passage does not make a judgment as to the actual capabilities of people who get selected for influential positions.

18. Answer choice B is correct. It discusses how a good thing is not put into practice because an aspect of the good thing is not good for the person (or people) who would put the good thing into practice. Answer choice A is incorrect because solutions to exam questions are not bad for a test taker. Answer choices C and D are incorrect because there is also no adverse consequence for a decision maker. Answer choice E is incorrect because a good decision is not impeded by an adverse aspect of the decision.

19. This question identifies three factors that it says should affect the use of military force: whether it affects innocent people, whether it affects aggressors, and whether it is expensive. Answer choice C is correct because it fully embraces two of those factors, the effect on aggressors and the expense, to conclude that military force is inappropriate. Answer choice A is incorrect because it embraces one of the factors (expense), and partially embraces a second factor (effect on aggressors). Answer choice B is incorrect because it also embraces one factor (expense) and partially embraces another factor (effect on aggressors). Answer choice D is incorrect because it also embraces one factor (expense) and partially embraces another factor (effect on aggressors). Answer choice E is incorrect because it completely embraces one factor (effect on innocent people) but does not wholeheartedly embrace another factor (affect on aggressors) because it does not tell us how many aggressors were affected.

20. A is correct because it deals a blow to Peter's argument. While in theory killing some people to save other people may sound attractive, such a theory would not be practical if answer choice A is true. Answer choice B is wrong because it does not address the circumstance in which, in the aggregate, people are not killed because certain people's death will save other people from death. Answer choice C is wrong because it is possible that in the future, with changes, the death penalty may save lives. This answer choice could be correct, but answer choice A is stronger. Answer choice A establishes that, without qualification as to what happened in the past, it is not possible to carry out what Peter argues. Answer choice D is incorrect because it does not have a bearing on the discussion between Peter and John. Answer choice E is incorrect because it does not address Peter's argument.

21. Answer choice D is correct because the passage establishes that bilingual people can learn to speak a third language with less of an accent. Answer choice A is incorrect because the motivation of people is not an issue touched on in the passage. Answer choice B is incorrect because the passage does not associate intelligence with an ability to speak languages. Rather, the passage cites the upbringing of people as a major factor that determines their linguistic ability. Answer choice C is incorrect because the passage only addresses the difference between people who speak one and two languages throughout their formative years. While answer choice C is a permissible conclusion from the facts of the passage, answer choice D is correct because it directly addresses the circumstance

in which a person knows two languages. Answer choice E is incorrect because the passage does not speak of strategies for acquiring languages.

22. Answer choice E is correct because it actually strengthens the teacher's reasoning. Not only will the classes make the team better, the team may also find them interesting and stimulating. Answer choice A is incorrect because it establishes the football field, and not the classroom, as a good place to teach football. Answer choice B is incorrect because it establishes how taking classes could contribute to losing games. Answer choice C is incorrect because it is not as strong as answer choice E. Answer choice C tacitly endorses classroom teaching, but answer choice E indicates that it is good for most teams. Answer choice D is incorrect because it establishes a shortcoming of using classroom instruction.

23. Answer choice A is correct because it concerns a key assumption made by the question. With a wider road, cars would go faster. But it is not clear that the road would be safer with faster cars. Answer choice B is incorrect because it is not as good an answer as answer choice A. Safety on a winding road is more closely linked to speed than it is to congestion. Answer choice C. is wrong because, while it could be correct, it does not address the critical assumption about speed and safety that is identified in answer choice A. Answer choice D is wrong because a wider road could be safer, even if more vehicles travel on it. Answer choice E is incorrect because it is too broad.

24. Answer choice B is correct because the author uses one aspect of the witnesses' account to completely discount everything they say. It is possible that the witnesses have consistent accounts of things other than the cause of the accident. Answer choice A is incorrect because answer choice B is a better answer. Whether there are other reasons to explain the different opinions does not by itself establish a flaw in the argument. The flaw exists because the author uses one fact (different opinions of witnesses) to arrive at a conclusion about everything the witnesses say. Answer choice C is incorrect because, like answer A, it seeks an explanation for the different opinions and does not itself identify the argument's flaw. Answer choice D is incorrect because it describes a consequence of the flawed reasoning, but does not itself identify the reasoning's flaw. Answer choice E is incorrect because it seeks a solution to the circumstance that gives rise to the flawed argument, but does not describe why the argument is flawed.

25. A is incorrect because whether this phrase is unclear does not affect the validity of the conclusion. B is incorrect because it attacks the facts, not the conclusion of this question. C is correct. It is uncertain whether "most people" are better able to evaluate the conduct of multinationals than are journalists. D is incorrect because the conclusion assumes that most people can better evaluate multinationals' activities, not that journalists are incapable of doing so. E is incorrect because nothing in this question provides a basis for comparing one multinational's activities to those of another.

26. Answer choice A is correct because if Mr. Lozano paints birds, he will place women in that painting. If he places women in the painting, he will not place men in the painting also. Thus, if Mr. Lozano paints birds, he does not also place men in the

painting. Answer choice B is incorrect because under the rules of the question there is nothing that prevents Mr. Lozano from placing women in paintings of cars. Answer choice C is incorrect because, while it is possible that the artist does not combine seascapes and birds, such a conclusion does not flow from the rules. Answer choice D is incorrect because Mr. Lozano can also paint men in seascapes. Answer choice E is incorrect because it is not a conclusion that must follow from the rules. The question indicates that the four kinds of subject matter are the artist's "basic kinds of subject matter". This does not extinguish the possibility that the artist also paints other kinds of subject matter.

SECTION IV: WAR GAMES

Questions 1 - 6
Here is the diagramming for the first war game that concerns questions 1 through 6:

spices
cu, s, b, p, o, ci

(cu, b, p → Ø)

② cu, s̶, b, p, o, c̶i̶

④ s, ci, p, cu

⑤ s/ci, sb, sp, so, s/cu
ci/b, ci/p, ci/o, ci/cu
p/cu

1.   A is correct because it is the only combination that is not prohibited by a rule. B and E are prohibited by the rule "When Mary uses oregano, she cannot also use paprika, cumin or basil." C is prohibited by the rule "Basil and cumin cannot be used together." And D is prohibited by "Basil and paprika cannot be used together."

2.   Here is the diagramming for this figure:

② cu, s̶, b, p, o, c̶i̶

All the spices are listed, with the prohibited spices crossed out. Once you write this out, you should look for which of the remaining spices can be used with another spice. Paprika and cumin can be used together, so any response choice that includes one of them will be incorrect. Thus, D and E are incorrect. The other answer choices basically allow us to choose between oregano, basil or oregano and basil. So, starting with answer choice A, we check to see if oregano can be used with something else. The rule "When Mary uses oregano, she cannot also use paprika, cumin or basil" tells us that oregano cannot be used with any of the remaining choices. Thus, either Answer choice A or C is correct. Next, we check to see whether basil can be used with another spice. From the above rule we know that basil cannot be used with oregano. From the rules "Basil and cumin cannot be used together" and "Basil and paprika cannot be used together" we know that basil cannot be used with either of the other two spices either. Thus, Answer choice C is correct.

3. In looking at all our rules and deductions, we do not see anything that prohibits the combinations listed in answer choices A and B. Answer choice C is correct because the rule "When Mary uses oregano, she cannot also use paprika, cumin or basil" eliminates three spices that can be used with oregano. That leaves only two spices that can be used with oregano. Thus, answer choice C is correct. Answer choice D is wrong because basil can be used with salt and cinnamon (it cannot be used with any other spice though). E is wrong because the rules only prohibit cumin from being used with basil and oregano. That leaves three other spices that it can be used with.

4. Here is the diagramming for this problem:

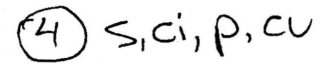

Answer choice A is wrong because, as we just saw in the problem above, Mary at most can use only two other spices with oregano. Answer choices B, D and E ask us to what are the most permissible combinations. Before we get to those related answer choices, let's look at answer choice C to see if we can eliminate it. The rules do not indicate that Mary must combine spices. Thus, she could use salt all by itself. Thus, answer choice C is wrong. To find the correct response among answer choices B, D and E we need to determine the greatest number of spices that can be used. To do this, we list out spices we believe would be in the largest group. We steer clear from oregano, because it eliminates many spices if it is used (it eliminates 3 of the 6 spices, leaving only 3 total permissible spices). We insert salt and cinnamon because no spice gets eliminated if they are used. Then, we see how we can add the most spices of the remaining ones, which are basil, paprika and cumin. By looking at the diagramming for these rules we can see that basil will eliminate both paprika and cumin:

But, in looking at all the rules, we can tell that paprika and cumin do not eliminate each other, so they both can be used. Paprika, cumin, salt and cinnamon add up to four spices. Now, let's double check to see if we were correct to not include oregano in our initial analysis. By using oregano, we would be able to use a total of 3 spices, but we know we can use four spices with a different combination. At this point, we know there are no combinations that will get us above four spices, so answer choice E is correct.

5. The diagramming for question 5 is:

$$⑤ \quad s/ci, \; sb, \; sp, \; so, \; s/cu$$
$$ci/b, \; ci/p, \; ci/o, \; ci/cu$$
$$p/cu$$

Here, the best approach is to simply list out all the potential combinations. The easiest way to do this is to start with one spice and list every permissible combination with that spice. Then, move on to another spice, and list all permissible combinations of that spice, without of course repeating combinations you have already listed. Here, I started by listing all the combinations with salt, and then listed all the combinations with cinnamon. I knew both of those do not have restrictions on what they can be combined with, so they simply can be combined with each of the other spices. Then, I looked to seek if there were any other permissible combinations not already listed, and only found paprika and cumin. Note that I put a long line between combinations, such as the "s" and "ci" combination, because I didn't want to be confused by "sci". When double checking my work, or looking back at that notation, it wouldn't be immediately clear to me what those letters represented. They could be "sc" and "i" or "sci". It would not be instantaneously clear to me that it would represent a salt and cinnamon combination. Once you list all the combinations, you add them up, and find that answer choice B is correct and all the rest are wrong. The answer choices are a little gracious here. If you were off by one and came up with 11 possible combinations, you would find that no answer choice fits that result, and that it must therefore be wrong. You could then go back and double check your work.

6. This difficult question is best approached by building on what you learned in question 5. In that question we listed all the possible combinations when two spices are used. To answer question 6 we need a solid handle on which combinations are permissible when 3 spices are being used.
    Now, let's eliminate answer choices. Answer choice A can be true, but does not have to be true and is thus incorrect. We can find a combination of three spices that does not include both salt and cumin. One such combination would be paprika, cumin and

cinnamon. Answer choice B is incorrect because Mary can use oregano, salt and cinnamon. Answer choice C is incorrect because Mary would not have to use cinnamon. She could use paprika, cumin and salt. Answer choice D is incorrect because Mary could use oregano, salt and cinnamon. Answer choice E is correct. A combination of three spices is impossible without either salt or cinnamon.

Questions 7 – 12.

Here is the diagramming for game 2, which concerns questions 7 - 12:

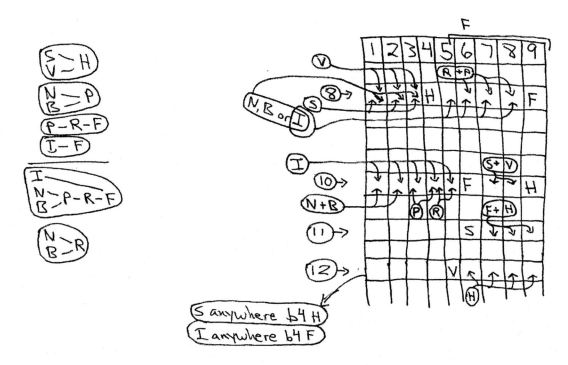

7.   From this diagram of deductions we know that at least five students must go before F:

Thus, answer choice A is incorrect. From this diagram we also know that at least three students must follow N, so N cannot be the seventh out of the nine children. Therefore, answer choice B is incorrect. C is incorrect for the same reason. At least three students must follow B. E is wrong because at least two students must follow P. D is correct. Only F must follow I, so I can be the eighth student out of the nine.

8. A number of rules come into play for this question, so it is helpful to look at the diagramming in the grid above by the circled number 8. As you can see from the grid, lots of people can be taught third under the facts of this question, but not everyone can. We simply need to find such person in the answer choices. Only answer choice B, which lists student R, provides an answer of someone with an arrow that does not connect to the third box.

9. From this diagram we know that at least five students must go before F:

Therefore, answer choice E is correct. No other rule, or deduction, eliminates any of the other choices.

10. As we have learned above, five students must go before F. Thus, if F is taught sixth, then all five preceding spaces will be taken up. We don't know the exact order of those students, but we do know they will all go in those five spaces. That leaves three spaces following F. From the rule "S and V are both taught before H" we know that H will have to be in the last of those three remaining spaces, which will be the ninth space. Thus, C is correct. None of the other answer choices are correct. Answer choice A is incorrect because, while we know that S must be before H, we do not know where it should be relative to V. Thus, S could be either 7th or 8th. The same kind of analysis applies to the other answer choices. We simply do not have enough information from which to conclude that the answer choices *must* be in the places indicated.

11. Here we can conclude that F and H must both be after S. We know H must be after S because a rule says so. F must be after S because five students other than S must be before F. There wouldn't be enough room for all five students if F were before S. What is tricky here is that there are many possible student combinations here. In the last three spaces alone here are *some* possibilities: F can go before or after H, V can go before or after F, or V doesn't have to be in the last three spaces and someone else (I or R) can go there. A is the correct response because P cannot be in the last three spaces. P must go before R and F. H and F must be in the last three spaces, and if R is placed in either the seventh or the eighth space, then there would be no room for P in those last three spaces. Thus, H must be after P. Rules or deductions do not support the other responses. There is no rule or deduction that establishes where V must be taught relative to F. Thus, B is wrong. The same is true for the other answer choices. If you look at the diagrams of the rules and deductions, you will notice that there is no hyphen that goes between students in the other answer choices (I-R, R-V, and N-B). Thus, we cannot determine their place with respect to each other.

12. Answer choice A is incorrect because it does not comply with this deduction:

Answer choice B is incorrect because B does not fit in one of the four spaces following V. H must go in one of those spaces, and three students must follow B. Answer choice C is incorrect for the same reason. N does not fit in one of the four last spaces. D is correct because P fits in one of the last four spaces. H can go in any one of those spaces, so P could be after H. E is incorrect because F must have at least five students, not including V, before F. If F is right after V, then there are only four free spaces before F.

Questions 13 – 18.
Here is the diagramming for game 3, which concerns questions 13 - 18:

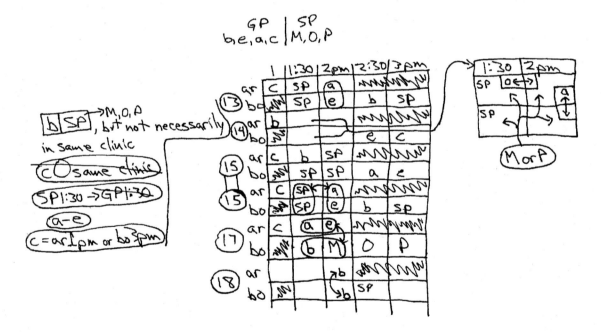

One important background item to note here is that there are a total of 7 doctors and only 7 time slots. All doctors see patients, so all slots must be filled.

13. Because a specialist sees a patient at 1:30, another specialist must also see a patient at 1:30. A is incorrect because Coopersman could be at 1 pm in Arsbald, and Ostwawill could be at 1:30 pm in Bodt.   B is incorrect because Barnerdale may see patients at 1 pm in Arsbald. C is incorrect because Artnarp could be scheduled at 1 pm without violating any rules. If Artnarp were scheduled at 1 pm, Coopersman would be at

3 pm and everyone else could be scheduled in between at appropriate times. Answer D is correct. If Barnerdale is at 2:30, then Coopersman must be at 1 pm (because a specialist must follow Barnerdale at 3 pm, and Coopersman is not a specialist). Specialists must both be in the 1:30 time slot , and that leaves only the 2 pm time slot for both clinics. Artnarp and Eavedorn must both go into those time slots, but that is not permissible under the rules. Artnarp must go before Eavedorn. Answer choice E is incorrect because Partnit may also be scheduled at 1:30.

14. This question calls for some complex diagramming because there are so many options. If Barnerdale is at 1 pm, then Coopersman must be at 3 pm. Because Barnerdale is at 1 pm, two specialists must be at 1:30 pm. This leaves only 2 and 2:30 for general practitioners. Because of that, Eavedorn must be in the 2:30 slot because she must be after Artnarp. This leaves a multiplicity of options for the 1:30 and 2 pm slots, which are diagramed above.

Because we know Eavedorn must be scheduled at 2:30 in Bodt, we can eliminate all answer choices that do not include her in that slot. Thus, answer choices B, D and E are wrong. C is wrong because Ostwawill cannot be scheduled in the same clinic as Coopersman. Coopersman is in Bodt, so Ostwawill cannot also be there. Only answer choice A does not violate any rule or deduction.

15. E is correct because it is the only answer choice with doctors that must see patients before 2:30 pm. For this question, plug in the doctors at 2:30 and see if you can get the entire scheduling to work. Here, if Barnerdale is at 2:30 a specialist will have to be at 3 pm. This means Coopersman must be at 1 pm. Two specialists and two general practitioners must be scheduled in the four remaining slots at 1:30 and 2 pm. However, if a specialist is at 1:30, then both of them must be at that time. If one specialist is at 2, then both must also be at that time. This does not allow for Artnarp to be scheduled before Eavedorn. Thus, Barnerdale cannot be at 2:30. Any answer choice that does not include Barnerdale is probably wrong, so we can eliminate answer choices A, D and D.

Artnarp cannot be scheduled at 2:30 either. If he is, then Eavedorn must be at 3 pm; then, Coopersman must be at 1 pm. That means all three specialists must be scheduled in the four remaining time slots at 1:30 and 2. Barnerdale must be before a specialist, so he would have to be at 1:30 pm. This would mean that a specialist would also have to be scheduled at 1:30 (that is one of the only three remaining slots), which is not permissible. A specialist cannot be scheduled at 1:30 together with a Barnerdale, who is a general practitioner.

16. Fortunately, question 16 is more straightforward. You can look at the answer choices and tick through the rules to see which choice complies with all the rules. Answer choice A is wrong because it would leave Ostwawill and Coopersman both in Bodt, which is impermissible under the rules. B is correct. Those three doctors could be in Arsbald and Marstervel, Artnarp, Ostwawill and Eavedorn could be the sequence of doctors in Bodt. Answer choice C is incorrect because it will not allow for Barnerdale to be scheduled before a specialist. D is incorrect because it will also not allow for Barnerdale to be scheduled before a specialist. Under the facts of D, Coopersman would have to be at 3 pm and Eavedorn would have to be at 2:30 pm in Bodt. Barnerdale could

not be at 1:30 because he is not a specialist. But, if he is at 2 pm he will not be before a specialist. E is wrong because it does not allow for Artnarp to be scheduled before Eavedorn. Artnarp cannot be at 1:30 because Ostwawill, a specialist, is at that time.

17. As we learned in a question above, neither Artnarp or Barnerdale may see patients at 2:30 pm, so answer choices A and B are wrong. If Partnit is at 3 pm, then Coopersman must be at 1 pm. Thus, D is incorrect. If Eavedorn is at 2:30 pm, then Artnarp would have to be at 2 pm. This would leave two specialists to be scheduled in the three remaining slots. It is not possible schedule those specialists and Dr. Barnerdale

18. If Barnerdale is at 2 pm, a specialist will have to be at 2:30 pm. Answer choice A is incorrect because we can find a place for Eavedorn that is different from 2:30 pm. She can be at 3 pm under the rules. B is correct. If a specialist sees patients at 3 pm, then Coopersman would have to be at 1 pm. Then, Artnarp would have to be at 1:30 pm and Eavedorn at 2 pm. This would leave the other 1:30 slot as the only time that a specialist could schedule patients. That is impermissible under the rules because Artnarp, a general practitioner, also must be at 1:30. C is incorrect because Coopersman may also see patients at 1 pm under the rules. D is incorrect because Barnerdale may see patients in either clinic. E is incorrect because Ostwawill may also see patients at 1:30.

Questions 19 – 23.
Here is the diagramming for game 4, which concerns questions 19 - 23:

19. A is wrong because Marcia's number of classes must be greater than Steve's number of classes. This necessarily means Marcia teaches either three or four classes. A rule indicates that if Steve teaches a class Alice may not teach it. Steve teaches two classes (electronics and woodworking), leaving only two classes for Alice (bricklaying and auto repair). Because that is only two classes for Alice, and Marcia must teach three

or four, they both cannot teach exactly the same courses as each other. B is wrong because there is a rule that says Marcia must teach more classes than Steve. C is correct. Wayne is not restricted by any of the rules or their deductions, and thus may teach whatever Alice teaches. D is wrong because there is a rule that says if Steve teaches a course, Alice may not teach the course. E is wrong because Alice can only teach up to two classes, and Ronald must teach three classes.

20. A is incorrect because, if Ronald and Marcia do not teach bricklaying, then all the other teachers must teach bricklaying (Valerie and four other teachers must teach bricklaying). This is impossible under the rules because neither Zeba nor Steve may teach what Alice teaches. Thus, those three cannot together teach bricklaying. In addition, Steve only teaches electronics and woodworking, not bricklaying. B is incorrect because it violates a rule. C is incorrect because, while it articulates a permissible schedule, that schedule does not *have to be* the schedule under the rules. D is correct. Alice must teach either auto repair or bricklaying, or both, because those are courses Steve does not teach, and Alice cannot teach whatever Steve teaches. E is incorrect because it violates a rule.

21. A is incorrect because, among other things, Valerie can teach bricklaying and auto repair. B is incorrect because it does not violate a rule. C is incorrect because, as we learned in the question above, Alice may teach one, or two, classes. Steve teaches two classes. D is incorrect because Marcia can teach three courses, which is what Ronald teaches. E is correct because, while Marcia must teach three or four classes, Alice may only teach up to two classes.

22. The critical deduction here is that Wayne must teach bricklaying because neither Steve nor Alice can teach that class. Because a total of five people must teach that class, then all five remaining of the seven teachers must teach bricklaying. Thus, B is correct. A is incorrect because there is not another class that Wayne must teach. C is incorrect because neither Valerie nor Wayne must teach only bricklaying. They may teach other classes that are different from what the other teaches. D is incorrect because bricklaying is the only class Wayne must teach. E is incorrect because, while Wayne and Marcia must teach bricklaying, there is not another class that Wayne must teach.

23. A is correct because there are no upper limits in the rules or deductions on the number of classes that Valerie, Wayne and Marcia can teach. B is incorrect because it is not a complete list. C is incorrect because Steve only teaches two classes and cannot teach a class that Alice teaches. D is incorrect because Zeba cannot teach a class that Alice teaches. E is incorrect because Alice cannot teach classes that Zeba or Steve teach.

Appendix F

Model Test Booklet

This booklet contains diagramming and other markings that a good test taker would make on the actual exam. To avoid confusion, none of the markings contain errors. Great test takers make mistakes and correct them.

The markings in this booklet are generally clearer than they would be on the booklet of many exam takers. Again, this is for clarity purposes. You do not need to have pencil markings as neat as those in this booklet because many people will not be reading your booklet. All that matters is that you understand your writing as you take the exam.

1. The Slenderhead fish in Spear Lake need oxygenated water to breathe and live healthy lives. The state electric authority recently granted Power Co. a permit to build a power plant close to the lake and use lake water to cool its turbines. Warm water from the plant will make algae grow and that algae will consume oxygen in the water, causing the level of oxygen in the lake to decline. The State has acted irresponsibly by endangering the future of the Slenderhead in Spear Lake.

The above conclusion depends on which of the following assumptions:

   (A) The power plant will cause the level of oxygen in the lake water to decline to levels at which Slenderhead fish may not be able to survive.

   (B) The State can act responsibly only if it denies Power Co. a permit to build a plant close to the lake.

   (C) Slenderhead fish are not an endangered species because they live in many other lakes.

   (D) Slenderhead fish are an endangered species that can only reproduce in Spear Lake.

   (E) Only the State, and not the Federal government, is responsible for the wellbeing of wildlife.

2. The effort expended by a human being running five miles per hour creates a noticeable level of fatigue in the muscles of the heart. Because specialized medical devices exist that can detect that fatigue, we will be able to screen out astronaut candidates that pose a risk of heart failure.

Which of the following most seriously weakens the argument?

   (A) Most people are unaware of any level of fatigue in their heart when they run at that speed.

   (B) The level of fatigue in heart muscles does not affect the risk of heart failure.

   (C) Other factors, such as intelligence, are more important in an astronaut.

   (D) In the past astronauts have not been screened with this technology.

   (E) Fatigue is only one factor that affects a person's likelihood of heart failure.

3. Expert: Conflict is often thought of as being destructive because it can impede cooperation among the conflicting parties. However, the benefits of conflict should not be overlooked because they have been substantial. Wars have not only served as catalysts for innovation, they have forged a unity that has led to a prosperity in nations that would not exist otherwise.

The main point of the above reasoning can best be expressed as:

   (A) Conflict is more beneficial than it is destructive.

   (B) Without conflict people become unproductively complacent.

   (C) If there were more conflict, there would be more prosperity.

   (D) Cooperation mixed with conflict is the optimum solution.

   (E) Conflict has been beneficial amidst destructive events.

4. Declaring bankruptcy is painful. It hinders a person's ability to obtain credit for many years and landlords may refuse to rent property. Personal debt burdens are harmful only if the debts cannot be paid for many years. Often, people find that if they work harder and live a simpler lifestyle they can make payments on their debts. Therefore, people should not declare bankruptcy unless there is simply no way they will be able to repay their debts.

Which of the following principles, if true, supports the above reasoning?

   (A) A process that is definitely painful should not be used to address a situation that can potentially be resolved.

   (B) Pain should be avoided with hard work.

   (C) It is better to be a good person than to live irresponsibly and depend on painful solutions.

   (D) Harmful circumstances can always be avoided with careful planning.

   (E) Long term solutions work best to address short term problems

GO OVER TO THE NEXT PAGE.

5. Chuck: Few people from the Ton Ton tribe have served on the council, despite the fact that many people from other tribes are on the council. Therefore, either Ton Ton tribe members are not as politically active as other tribes, or the council has unfairly excluded them.

Mary: The Ton Ton tribe is small compared to other tribes that are several times its size. Thus, it is possible that there are proportionately more Ton Ton members on the council than there are members of other tribes.

Which of the following most closely describes Mary's response?

(A) She establishes that the groups Chuck compares do not have significant commonalities.
(B) She uses competing data to question Chuck's conclusion.
(C) She uses information that undermines the accuracy of Chuck's information.
(D) She calls into question Chuck's conclusion by establishing that he uses absolute numbers instead of proportions.
(E) She demonstrates Chuck has improperly defined the groups he compares.

6. The use of diets as the primary method of strengthening the body is a misguided approach to fitness. The focus should be on exercise. The body is able to convert foods of average nutritional value into the many kinds of nutrients it needs. However, the body does not generate muscle in the absence of exercise. Exercise is therefore critical and should be the main focus of a wellness routine.

Which of the following most strengthens the above argument?

(A) Most diets do not work because people who are on them don't make an effort to exercise.
(B) Through exercise the body not only increases muscle tissue, but also increases its ability to convert food into needed nutrients.
(C) The dieting industry is so filled with questionable "easy, no pain" solutions that it is best not to even try to find a useful diet.
(D) Exercise makes you more hungry, making it less necessary to diet.
(E) Celebrities who succeeded the most have strong bodies, but do not promote diets.

7. Student: A university education is something that certain successful people have, but not all successful people have a university education. Furthermore, there are people who attended a university, and who even obtained good grades, who are not successful. Thus, a university education does not create successful people.

The student's reasoning is most clearly called into question by the fact that it:

(A) provides a questionable justification for not being industrious.
(B) is narrow in its focus on "success" in life, when there are many other things worth striving for.
(C) concludes that a link between education and success does not exist because it does not always exist.
(D) ignores the fact that unsuccessful university graduates may be unsuccessful for reasons not related to their education.
(E) is limited in its analysis of university graduates when there is a huge variety of education levels.

8. Modern art represents a substantial increase in the creative bandwidth available to artists. Unlike past art forms, such as Impressionism and artistic styles used during the Renaissance, modern art is not bound by the forms, shapes or colors that are found in scenes observed in nature. Modern art has the potential to fully unleash the creative energy of artistic minds.

The argument's main conclusion is best stated as being:

(A) Modern art allows for a greater variety of expression than prior art forms.
(B) Freedom of expression is the most important factor for identifying good art.
(C) Modern art is better, even if it is harder to understand than other forms of art.
(D) Good art is a matter of taste in the eye of the beholder, not in the freedom of the artist.
(E) Prior art forms would have been better if they allowed for more freedom of expression.

GO OVER TO THE NEXT PAGE.

135

9. Eating spicy chicken can cause stomach cramps in people that are not used to eating spicy food. While Bob was on a long trip he got stomach cramps and was not able to relax. Bob must have eaten spicy chicken, or at least some spicy food.

The conclusion is vulnerable to the criticism that:

(A) It changes its use of "cramps" from "discomfort" to "inability to relax."
(B) It considers one event that can cause a second event as being necessary for the occurrence of the second event.
(C) It uses irrelevant information to support its reasoning.
(D) It uses an overbroad rule to arrive at the conclusion.
(E) It ignores the possibility that Bob was eating unfamiliar food.

10. Books printed with new technology have an average of only 2 defects for every 10 books printed. With two quality inspections a printing company can deliver a thousand books with a total of only 15 defects. Therefore, it is cost effective to do just two quality inspections for most books.

This reasoning is most susceptible to critique on which of the following grounds?

(A) It fails to consider the fact that it is possible that all defects would be detected with one additional inspection.
(B) The cost of defects can be huge because customers for some books become extremely upset when they see even one defect.
(C) The author arrives at the conclusion without weighing the costs and benefits of additional improvements.
(D) Some books are really expensive to print, so it is better to print them right rather than to do a quality check later.
(E) Investment in even better printing technology will improve books more than spending more on quality control.

11. Squeaks and rattling can be heard in some cars that have been on rough roads, or that have run over a sudden bump at a high speed on the freeway. Those noises can be indications that the car will become unsafe, such as if a piece of the drivetrain is loose, or if the braking system is becoming undone. However, all cars develop noises as they age, and such noises are not always indications of danger. The same is true of cars that have been on rough roads.

The conclusion of the above statements can best be expressed as:

(A) Newer cars are safer than cars that have squeaks and rattling.
(B) In general, cars that have been on rough roads are less safe than other cars.
(C) People should pay attention to the maintenance needs of their car so that noises do not develop.
(D) Squeaks and rattling in a car that has been on rough roads are not necessarily indications of danger.
(E) Rough roads should be avoided because they are harder on your car than other roads.

12. Student: The island of Tikilaka is a good place to take a vacation because all my friends who have been there loved it. All major cruise lines regularly dock in its harbor and every major airline has flights to its busy airport.

The above reasoning assumes that:

(A) The friends who have gone to Tikilaka can accurately assess whether the island is a good vacation destination.
(B) Tikilaka's busy harbor and airport do not distract from the fact that the island is a good place to take a vacation.
(C) The friends who have gone to Tikilaka were there on vacation.
(D) The views of the friends who have been to Tikilaka are representative of people who have visited that island.
(E) Tikilaka's airport and harbor are busy because of the tourism industry.

GO OVER TO THE NEXT PAGE.

13. Activist: Immigrants from African countries to the United States have, relative to the general American population, a disproportionately low level of advanced degrees. This is further evidence of racial discrimination by the white majority establishment against black African immigrants.

If true, which of the following most seriously calls into question the above conclusion?

    (A) African immigrants have less education when they immigrate than the general American population.

    (B) African immigrants have a higher proportion of advanced degrees than the people in their countries of origin.

    (C) White immigrants from Eastern Europe also have a disproportionately low level of advanced degrees.

    (D) Asian immigrants pursue advanced degrees more vigorously than do immigrants from other regions.

    (E) The American population maintains its vitality with the influx of ambitious immigrants seeking a better future.

14. Researcher: A recent study concluded that most cancers cannot be prevented by good eating habits. The study found that people who eat a healthy diet die of cancer at a higher rate than other people. However, people who eat a healthy diet live longer than other people, and the incidence of cancer rises in older people regardless of what diet they follow.

The researcher's main point can best be described as:

    (A) People should be encouraged to eat a healthy diet because a balanced intake of nutrients is good for you.

    (B) The study's conclusion about healthy eating is called into question by the incidence of cancer in elderly people.

    (C) The study is flawed because healthy eating is obviously good for you, even if it may have some bad side effects.

    (D) If you want to live a long life, you should eat a healthy diet and prepare yourself for the ailments that will afflict you later in life.

    (E) A healthy diet does not have any adverse consequences, and the study's conclusion to the contrary is the result of incomplete analysis.

15. Teacher: To be a good leader you first have to know how to be a good follower. Many leaders ignore this concept and, in doing so, are ineffective because they do not appreciate how their actions will resonate with their followers. Only good leaders have good followers, because it is not possible to be a good follower of a bad leader.

Which of these must also be true if the Teacher's conclusions are correct?

    (A) Good leaders are hard to come by because most people would rather follow someone else, even if that person is a bad leader.

    (B) Leadership, whether good or bad, is acquired only through experience and is not the product of natural ability.

    (C) To overcome the shortcomings of your leaders you must seek to be more effective by being sensitive to how your actions resonate with others.

    (D) If someone is a good leader, then at some point they were a follower of another good leader from whom they learned good leadership.

    (E) People who believe they are good leaders should first consider whether their leaders were effective.

16. Though the reason for why they cure people has never been fully understood, herbal extracts have been a part of alternative medicine treatments for millennia. But, with advances in herbal extract testing techniques and the decoding of ancient medical texts that describe how certain extracts were discovered, modern medicine will now be able to understand and cooperate closely with people who practice alternative medicine.

The above argument depends on the following assumption:

    (A) Understanding and cooperation are possible, even if discoveries about the extracts challenge modern medicine's views of alternative medicine.

    (B) Modern medicine cannot cooperate closely with alternative medicine if it does not understand how herbal extracts work.

    (C) Herbal extracts are a significant part of alternative medicinal treatments.

    (D) The reasons herbal extracts cure people will be discovered and accepted by modern medicine.

    (E) Herbal extracts do in fact cure people.

GO OVER TO THE NEXT PAGE.

17. Chacho: Young parents in a survey indicated that they do not usually sleep well because their children wake them up constantly. Couples without children reported that they are generally healthy and relaxed. Having children does not enhance the well-being of parents because parents with children reported lower levels of wellness than other couples.

Lani: But children often take care of their parents when they are unable to care for themselves.

Of the following, which best describes Lani's response to Chacho's argument?

(A) She indicates that Chacho is correct, but for a different reason.
(B) It establishes a flaw in the survey's methodology.
(C) It offers information that calls into question Chacho's conclusion.
(D) Lani indicates Chacho assumes his conclusion is true.
(E) Lani argues Chacho's conclusion is incorrect because he did not consider important information.

18. Economist: The substantial drop in labor costs during the last quarter was highly beneficial for the economy because it helped make goods cheaper for everybody. If goods were not cheaper, the economy would not have expanded, and the country would instead have gone into a deep recession. Therefore, the drop in labor costs kept the country out of recession.

The economist's argument can be called into question because:

(A) it does not consider the possibility that lower labor costs mean lower wages for poor working people
(B) it does not consider the possibility that goods may have gotten cheaper even without lower labor costs
(C) it does not take into account the many factors that go into the analysis of a country's economy
(D) economists, unlike investors, only analyze data about the past and do not seek to predict the future
(E) cheaper goods are only one of many different ways that an economy can be stimulated, and kept out of a recession

19. As the computer revolution has progressed the amount of space and money required for computing power has decreased dramatically. In the earlier stages of the computer industry, this increase in efficiency allowed consumers to own a computer for entertainment purposes. In the industry's later stages, the more complex tasks required by small businesses could be accomplished by a computer purchased by a consumer.

Which of the following best articulates the information about the computer industry presented above?

(A) The increases in computing efficiency have empowered consumers to do more with computers they purchase.
(B) In the future big businesses will operate on computers used by consumers.
(C) The positive influence of the decline in the price for computing power is only now being fully realized.
(D) It is unlikely that in the future the computer revolution will be able to progress as much as it has in the past.
(E) It is a good idea for most consumers to take advantage of the many things they can now do with computers.

GO OVER TO THE NEXT PAGE.

138

20. In today's business environment trade secrets are more important than they have ever been in the past. The beverage industry, where the precise mixture of ingredients for a beverage can be a company's biggest asset, is a prime example of that reality. Only if the exact original recipe is followed can a beverage with the same fizz, sweetness and freshness be made.

If the above is true, which of these CANNOT be correct?

(A) Many additional beverages remain to be discovered, and that is why the existing trade secrets do not impede consumer choice.

(B) Companies maintain extensive procedures and controls to protect their recipes from competitors.

(C) Some beverage combinations, which have become widely used and highly profitable, were discovered by accident.

(D) With modern technology chemists are able to study beverages and come to conclusions about their makeup.

(E) Someone has, through research, made an exact reproduction of another company's secret beverage.

21. While gambling can be destructively addictive, it also has healthy entertainment value and can boost the economy of the area in and around a city with a gambling industry. To boost the economy and wellness of its citizens, the national legislature should promote gambling that has healthy entertainment value.

The above argument depends on the assumption that:

(A) It is possible to promote gambling in a manner that, on balance, improves the life of citizens.

(B) The entertainment value of gambling outweighs its destructive addictiveness.

(C) The improved economic conditions in gambling cities do not come at the expense of other communities.

(D) On a national scale, people want to gamble.

(E) The life of citizens can be improved through promoting gambling more so than through promoting anything else.

22. Commercial: Buy Timber Trucks because they are better than other trucks. A recent study found Timber Trucks are cheaper and used less gas on average than other trucks in their class. Farmer George has been using Timber Trucks for over 30 years and says "I would not trade my truck for anything."

All of the following establish a reason to question the commercial EXCEPT:

(A) The facts presented were not compiled by an independent source.

(B) An older Timber Truck could be hard to purchase.

(C) A general conclusion about Timber Trucks is arrived at based on limited criteria.

(D) The durability of the Timber Truck compared to other trucks is not established.

(E) No facts concerning the safety of the trucks are considered.

GO OVER TO THE NEXT PAGE

139

23. Advertisement: Using doctor recommended Handlea cream regularly is the best way to make you appear younger because it makes wrinkles on your face disappear. Studies have repeatedly shown that people who use Handlea cream are perceived to be younger than their actual age.

For this to be an effective advertisement:

(A) The studies cited must be accurate, even though the people studied may not have used the cream regularly.
(B) There must be no better way to get rid of wrinkles.
(C) Readers with wrinkles must want to appear younger.
(D) Readers must trust what is said, even though it is an advertisement.
(E) Having a young appearance is a good thing.

24. The seashell deposits on Point Lalton, a popular tourist attraction, have fluctuated over the years. A storm can wash large quantities of seashells on to the point's beaches, where tourists pick out the brighter and more colorful shells. Sometimes currents around the point shift and erode accumulations of shells. Seashell deposits on Point Lalton are at an all time low, so a storm will surely sweep over the point soon.

The above reasoning assumes that:

(A) The level of seashell deposits on the point is related to the probability of a storm sweeping through the point.
(B) Storms do not assail the point when it has large seashell deposits.
(C) Low levels of seashell deposits cause storms on Point Lalton.
(D) Shifting currents that erode seashell deposits signal a change to a weather pattern that will cause a storm.
(E) Tourists have not removed a significant number of seashells from the point.

GO OVER TO THE NEXT PAGE.

140

25. To maintain a high level of speed during the entire Sparkling Diamond race, cars must stop to refuel at least three times. Racer Rob refueled only twice, but was first place in the race.

Which of the following explains the above outcome?

(A) Racer Rob is an experienced driver with an advanced car.
(B) An accident in the beginning of the race eliminated all contestants except for Racer Rob.
(C) It is _possible_ to finish the race faster by not operating at a high level of speed and avoiding one refuel stop.
(D) Not all cars have the same level of fuel efficiency.
(E) Technique, not just high levels of speed, can win a race.

26. A liberal arts education is more desirable than a technical degree for most of society's workers because, with it, students can apply core concepts to a wide variety of career paths. Courses leading to a technical degree often do not teach core concepts, and instead focus on specific sequences of tasks that will become obsolete as technology and the economy change.

If valid, which of these provides the strongest justification for the above reasoning?

(A) Some of the most successful people in society have liberal arts degrees and report no interest in getting a technical degree.
(B) Core concepts are more interesting, but more complex, than task sequences.
(C) Workers' versatility because of their ability to apply core concepts substantially increases their well-being.
(D) Jobs of a technical nature can be easily outsourced to other countries.
(E) Liberal arts degree graduates have a higher IQ than technical degree graduates.

S T O P

141

The Mayas were a peace loving people until the Toltec influence appeared in their culture. The Mayas, though best known for their main pyramid at Chichen Itzá, were also avid sports enthusiasts. They played a game that is a precursor to modern basketball.

In this game, small hoops are attached high on the wall of a large courtyard. The players were allowed to use only their waist and ankles to touch the ball. Scoring was extremely difficult for that reason, and because the ball was only a little smaller than the hoops.

This sport provided a means for defusing tensions among subgroups of the Maya, the same way that modern sports do. However, that changed when the Toltecs arrived. This sport, rather than defusing tension, became an instrument for creating discord. The rules changed so that the captain of the losing team would get killed. This transformed the game into a battle of life and death, with an important person's life at stake. The deaths of such important people probably created resentment and hatred that would spill over into violence outside the game. This would be especially true if the outcome of the game was disputed. The effect of a bad call by the game's referee would be disastrous.

While the brutality of such a game is undeniable, it appears that participation in the game was voluntary. For religious reasons, or to acquire fame, players themselves enabled the violence. Thus, one can hardly feel sorry for the captains who lost their lives. They not only agreed to the process that killed them, but they made the process possible.

The victims of the violence that resulted from the sport however, were innocent. Their blood rests on the heads of the athletes and of the Toltecs.

It is difficult to arrive at definite conclusions about this game however, because we do not have a definite historical record about it. The Mayan civilization declined and the sport ceased to be played by the time the Spanish arrived. Shortly after their arrival, the Spanish destroyed almost all records pertaining to Mayan history.

What have survived, however, are the game courts. They have been reconstructed after the hoops alongside them had fallen off. The trees and shrubs that had overgrown the courts have been uprooted and grass once again grows in them. Some of the old game courts' acoustics are surprisingly good. At the court of Chichen Itzá, people can stand at the ends of the court, which is at least 80 feet long, and talk to each other as if they were standing next to one another.

While the game was a source of death in its day, today it is a lifeblood for the local economy. Tourists spend several million dollars a year visiting the ruins and enjoying Mayan hospitality.

1. The author probably believes:

(A) A lot of people died because of the game.
(B) The Spanish were more violent than the Toltecs.
(C) Mayan civilization declined because of the game.
(D) Toltecs played the game better than the Mayas
(E) The game's new rules were not just.

2. Which of the following best describes the tone of the passage:

(A) Indignation because of injustice.
(B) Balanced historical analysis.
(C) Confusion over a lack of information.
(D) Impassioned advocacy for the rights of the oppressed.
(E) Hopefulness for a better future.

GO OVER TO THE NEXT PAGE.

3. From this passage we can conclude:

   (A) Games are the most effective way to defuse social tension.
   (B) The Mayas were conquered by the Toltecs.
   (C) The game was entertaining.
   (D) The Mayas would have been better off discontinuing the game.
   (E) Most games were probably unfair because the stakes were so high.

4. The information about the Spanish is included to:

   (A) Qualify the statements made about the game's victims.
   (B) Place blame on the Spanish for the decline of the game.
   (C) Clarify why the Mayan civilization declined.
   (D) Explain why historical research is important.
   (E) Indicate a possible solution to the puzzle created by an incomplete historical record.

5. The passage is most consistent with the witch of the following statements:

   (A) Peoples of the past were more violent than those of the present.
   (B) Justice is served when there is a constructive mechanism for defusing social tension.
   (C) Games that involve death are always wrong.
   (D) We do not have enough information about the game to learn a lesson about it.
   (E) Modern sports at times can have the same problems that this game had.

GO OVER TO THE NEXT PAGE

143

Income inequality is generally bad for a nation because it breeds violence, envy, and mistrust. Even if everyone in a society has enough wealth to live what most would consider a "normal comfortable life," people do not feel "normal" when they live in proximity to really wealthy people. Thus, they perceive themselves as being "poor" even though they may not be poor by an objective measure. This perception, though flawed, breeds violence, corruption and other social ills.

Having a society with complete equality has proven unworkable. Because people have different abilities, they inevitably acquire different levels of wealth over time. Thus, wealth would have to be periodically rebalanced even if it were spread equally at any point in time.

Also, there are some benefits to inequality. Certain good things, like substantial investments in new technology, require lots of money. While governments can, and often do, make such investments, they do not necessarily have the skills to do so for all potential new technological advances. A highly skilled wealthy person can sometimes accomplish complex things, like the invention of a new computer, that a government bureaucracy cannot do.

Thus, to maximize the total wealth created by humanity, a balance must be struck between having some inequality and not having any inequality. This is an extremely difficult task because it is almost impossible to identify which skilled people, if given wealth, would multiply the wealth. The most we can hope for is a somewhat random distribution of assets within a range of inequality. As crime rises and economic growth stalls, the government should implement wealth redistribution programs. Such redistribution will greatly benefit wealthy people. Aside from the obvious benefit of lower crime, there are other benefits. With more widely available resources, business and technological advances occur more often. Wealthy people benefit from those advances, such as better software, safer cars, and better medicines. Having less money is by itself beneficial for many wealthy people because wealth can create, rather than avoid, problems. With more wealth, there is more to manage, and also more things that can go wrong.

Most politicians focus on increases and decreases in inequality. A more constructive focus would be to study what the wealth gets spent on. That way, if wealthy people generate the most wealth with their wealth, then increasing inequality may be a good thing. Giving more money to the middle class so they can take more vacations and buy bigger televisions is not necessarily in society's best interest.

Too often, popular attitudes are shaped by images from extreme ends of the spectrum. People think of inequality in terms of the super rich in their yachts and mansions benefiting at the expense of poor people with no housing or food. Those attitudes are fed by

sensationalism in the media, which focuses on dramatic subjects in the hope of attracting readership.

What is needed is careful analysis of how existing wealth is being used to generate additional wealth. Radical wealth redistribution based on sensationalist stories could actually decrease the overall level of wealth and the overall welfare of humanity.

6. Based on the passage, which of the following best describes the author's attitude towards the poor:

    (A) Irresponsible.
    (B) Mistrustful.
    (C) Sympathetic.
    (D) Insensitive.
    (E) Detached.

7. The main point of the passage can best be articulated as being:

    (A) Wellbeing and wealth are the same thing; therefore, social policy should seek to maximize both.
    (B) Inequality should exist within a certain range because it is difficult to know how much inequality is beneficial.
    (C) The media is irresponsible because it distorts the issues, thereby causing more inequality.
    (D) It is not possible to have an appropriate policy regarding wealth because the subject matter is too complicated.
    (E) Maximizing wealth, while difficult to do, can be accomplished if people are rewarded for their efforts.

GO OVER TO THE NEXT PAGE.

144

8. The author would most likely agree with a <u>wealth redistribution plan</u> that:

(A) Gives more money to the rich if they will not buy a yacht with it.

(B) Takes money from the poor if they do not spend it on things that are beneficial for them, such as food and housing.

(C) Creates a wealth allocation similar to an allocation that has created substantial wealth in the past.

(D) Does not give money to the middle class, because they usually do not spend their money in a manner that creates wealth.

(E) The author would not agree to any wealth redistribution plan.

9. The passage indicates that:

(A) Inequality is a good thing because complete equality is unworkable.

(B) Rebalancing wealth is too much work.

(C) Wealth redistribution can have non-monetary benefits.

(D) Taking many vacations is a bad thing.

(E) The media consciously misinforms the public about inequality.

10. The author lists the <u>benefits of inequality</u> in the third paragraph to:

(A) Create a distorted picture of the issue of wealth allocation that will lend support an erroneous conclusion about inequality.

(B) Offend the reader and create a distraction that will hide the serious flaws in the reasoning process through which inequality is not just accepted, but justified.

(C) Call into question commonly held beliefs about the wealthy and the management of society's resources.

(D) Articulate a view about how the wealthy expend resources that will lend support to the author's suggested course of action.

(E) Offer reasoning that, while questionable, is nonetheless plausible if you accept certain of the author's assumptions.

11. The views expressed in this passage are most beneficial to:

(A) Skilled people who can convince policymakers that they will use their skills to create substantial wealth if they are given much wealth.

(B) People with wealth who try to generate substantial wealth with the resources that they currently have.

(C) Poor people because they benefit the most from policies that attempt to increase the wealth for all humanity.

(D) Middle-class people because if they follow the views in this passage they will spend their money on things that really matter.

(E) Wealthy people, because the passage justifies inequality and thereby empowers wealthy people to accumulate more wealth.

12. The <u>primary purpose</u> of the passage is to:

(A) Explain why there are not many things that can be done to increase humanity's wealth.

(B) Describe factors that should be considered by policymakers making decisions about wealth allocation.

(C) Criticize the way in which wealth allocation is thought of by most people who read the media.

(D) Further the interests of wealthy skilled people who take credit for advances that would have been made anyway.

(E) Boost the amount of money that everyone can spend by postulating a formula for wealth allocation that the government can follow.

GO OVER TO THE NEXT PAGE.

The welfare of women has not necessarily increased over time according to the findings of Dr. Norma Casper. While the earnings and career opportunities of women have generally increased in the industrialized world, the demands on women have also increased. For women to have a career, they must obtain an education. The time and money that they must expend to simply graduate from some of the most glamorous careers, such as law and medicine, is substantial. Most women do not get married or have a family during the time they study for such professions. After they graduate, those professions become even more demanding.

Dr. Casper believes that the "progress" that has been made by women has only furthered the interests of men. Because there are more women doctors, the quality of medical care is higher and its cost is lower than it would be otherwise. Women have not been compensated for those increases in welfare, and have in fact made deep sacrifices. As a practical matter, women doctors often cannot have children, or do not have as many children and leisure time as they would have had otherwise, because of the time pressures imposed by their profession.

While the status of women in industrialized nations is somewhat complex, it is clear that in the rest of the world women continue to be abused. For the most part, women have not been allowed to participate in professions that are respected and that are pathways to power. The effect of having a weak legal system means that physical violence against women occurs with no consequence.

A solution to this situation is complicated by the fact that women themselves are often the biggest perpetrators of the injustice that they suffer from. In a survey by Dr. Casper, a majority of women indicated that they look to men for leadership in their romantic relationships. The oppressed thus reinforce the power of the oppressors. What is remarkable is that this oppression has existed for as long as there have been historical records. Nowhere has there ever been a free society that can serve as a model for the treatment of women. Studying the welfare of men is not helpful because, even though men have for the most part been free, their freedom has been obtained at the expense of women. Men, women, and history do not provide even a starting point for formulating an approach that would increase the welfare of women. Even if such an approach were found, it could not be implemented because men are in control and will not cede that control. This is especially true of approaches that have been formulated without the input of men.

Most sociologists find Dr. Casper's studies disturbing. They believe the findings are not scientific because Dr. Casper does not assign a numerical value to the postponement of marriage and other matters that the findings identify as "sacrifices."

13. The author would most likely agree with this statement:

(A) A distribution of wealth that follows innovative techniques for identifying deserving women that have succeeded in professions.

(B) Discrimination against women by men is the primary reason humanity is not as well off as it could be.

(C) Many women have had their views about equality influenced adversely by men and by a history of the past that distorts the welfare of women.

(D) Men do not realize the burdens they place on women when they expect so many things from them.

(E) Even well-intentioned people can be oppressive towards themselves if they do not have the right guidance.

14. The passage indicates that the current condition of women is the product of:

(A) A long process that, while not completely understood because of its ubiquity, is widely accepted.

(B) Misconceptions about progress that have in fact lead to the overall decline in social welfare and the disintegration of the family.

(C) A calculated and coordinated effort by men to maintain their social status at the expense of others, including women.

(D) The hope that women could achieve freedom by engaging in the oppressive acts that have brought men a measure of freedom.

(E) A system in which the condition of women is sought to be improved by industrializing nations so that they have more wealth.

GO OVER TO THE NEXT PAGE.

146

15. The author includes the views of most sociologists to:

(A) discredit Dr. Casper
(B) give a balanced view
(C) show an alternative approach
(D) highlight an issue
(E) qualify Dr. Casper's comparisons

16. The author's main purpose is to:

(A) expose the shortcomings of a radical theory by giving a number of examples in which it doesn't work and by explaining why it does not follow acceptable analytical steps for modern scientific inquiry.
(B) explore avenues for formulating an acceptable theory of social equality by describing shortcomings of the historical approach and the current approach taken by other theories.
(C) help women and encourage social change by reporting the highlights of significant and groundbreaking research that calls into question our basic understanding of the world.
(D) describe, with the help of scholarly research, how a number of commonly held views of women are not true and give a number of examples to support that conclusion.
(E) showcase Dr. Casper's finding that it is not possible to find a solution to the adverse treatment of women by using the scientific method, studying history, or other common approaches.

17. The purpose of the second paragraph is to:

(A) show how the medical profession in particular abuses women
(B) explain how an apparent good thing has in fact produced bad consequences
(C) indicate how the male conspiracy to oppress women has infiltrated an admired profession
(D) give an example of a failed approach in which even intelligent people were misled
(E) lay a factual basis from which a solution to the problem will naturally follow

18. Dr. Casper probably believes that:

(A) A solution to the problem she has studied is difficult to arrive at for more than one reason.
(B) It is not important to articulate her findings in numerical terms.
(C) If women were better off, everyone would be better off.
(D) Leadership is a form of wealth when it comes to comparing genders.
(E) Women should take responsibility for their actions by not getting into bad situations.

19. Under the reasoning in the passage, the relationship between men and women can best be described as:

(A) troubled, because women have not taken the initiative to do what is right for them
(B) damaged beyond repair because of long lasting discord
(C) less beneficial for women than it should be in light of what women do
(D) complicated such that unraveling its intricacies is probably not helpful
(E) something that may improve as technology advances

GO OVER TO THE NEXT PAGE

147

A political action group called Green Citizens is proposing legislation that would change how rights to water from the Clear Blue River would be allocated. Currently, farmers along the river use the water to irrigate their fields. Each farmer has a right to a certain amount of water that is based on the size of their property. If a farmer does not use their total water allotment, then nobody is allowed the use of the unused amount. This system has existed for several decades and is critical to the continuing success of the stable farm community along the river.

The Green Citizens have identified a number of problems with this system, and claim that those problems would be solved with a system in which rights to water are sold to the highest bidder. Of particular concern for the Citizens is their belief that the water can be more productively used for things other than farming. Water taken out of the river for irrigation lowers the level of the river. Some of that water washes back into the river with high concentrations of pesticides. The river is thus not able to have the wildlife that it would have without irrigation. If the rights to that water could be sold, the Citizens would buy them to enable wildlife to flourish in the river.

Farmers along the river are divided on the Citizens' proposed legislation. Some believe that the sale of their water rights will generate a substantial amount of money. They could use such money to invest in businesses that do not require irrigation. Other farmers are opposed to the legislation because they believe it will destabilize their community. These farmers are concerned that over time a substantial number of farmers along the river will sell the rights to their water. If that happens, farming will cease to be a viable business for the remaining farmers. Dealerships for farming equipment, and other businesses that support the farming industry, will no longer operate in the area because there will not be a critical mass necessary for such businesses.

In an unusual alliance, real estate developers have joined forces with the Green Citizens. These developers see a unique opportunity that would be created if the legislation passes. If the land along the river no longer had rights to the water, that land would be cheaper. If the river had more water, and thus more wildlife, it would be a more attractive place for people to live on its banks. Subdivisions could be placed along the river and the homes in them could be sold at a substantial profit. The developers would need to purchase some water permits to supply water to their developments, but those water needs would not be as much as is needed to irrigate the same amount of land.

Clear Blue University has performed a study on the probable effects of the proposed legislation, the conclusion of which is that the legislation is unnecessary. The developers could achieve their purposes by simply buying the existing land, using some of the water for residential purposes, and leaving the remaining water to nourish the wildlife.

20. The author would most likely agree with which of these statements:

(A) farming is not as productive as it once was along the river
(B) a new system for allocating water may be beneficial, but must be closely studied
(C) the correct solution will not be enacted because most voters are not farmers
(D) development of land along the river would only be marginally beneficial
(E) the current system should be kept because the proposed legislation will not change anything

21. If the legislation passes and a large industrial corporation buys a substantial amount of water rights for use in an activity that will pollute the river more than the current farming industry does, which of the following is the most persuasive reason for enjoining such activity through a court proceeding?

(A) The industrial activity will have a negative impact on land values along the river.
(B) Wildlife and farmers down river will be adversely affected by the pollution.
(C) Developers will have a harder time profiting from the sale of homes along the river.
(D) The pollution will be disruptive to the stable farm community that depends on the river.
(E) The purpose of the legislation was to reduce pollution, not to enable more pollution.

GO OVER TO THE NEXT PAGE.

148

22. The passage supports the following <u>conclusions</u> about the river, EXCEPT:

    (A) It is a significant factor that affects the current and potential wellbeing of the economy of the land that it runs through.

    (B) Wildlife that depends on the river can be protected under the current legal framework that establishes water rights.

    (C) It is possible that the water in the river is not as pure as it should be when the welfare of the wildlife and the surrounding community are all taken into account.

    (D) The full economic potential of the river may not be realized if the water rights are not separated from the ownership rights of the land along the river.

    (E) The existing farming community should be preserved, even if that means that other beneficial activities by the river must be foregone.

23. The passage establishes which of the following with respect to the <u>Green Citizens</u>:

    (A) They are a group of narrow minded people who do not have a stake in the existing economy that depends on the river.

    (B) Skepticism with respect to their approach is proper because they have taken on an issue that is more complex than they realize.

    (C) Its members are selfish because they want to change the river water rights in a manner that is beneficial to them, regardless of the consequences.

    (D) They seek to implement change in a manner that does not force existing stakeholders to give up their rights in the short term.

    (E) Development is something that should generally be opposed because restoring nature to its original condition is a higher goal.

24. The author included in the <u>last paragraph</u> to:

    (A) call into question the usefulness of the proposed legislation

    (B) indicate that the developers are dishonest in their support of the legislation

    (C) critique the reasoning of the Green Citizens

    (D) outline an alternative approach that others have not considered

    (E) challenge assumptions of the legislation in light of conditions along the river

25. The <u>author's attitude</u> towards the proposed legislation is most accurately described as:

    (A) convinced that it will pass, but cautious about whether it will be helpful

    (B) convinced that it will pass, but not supportive of its goals

    (C) largely indifferent towards the legislation, and sympathetic towards the farmers

    (D) convinced that it will not pass, but hopeful that a better solution will be found

    (E) convinced that it will not pass, and indifferent towards the consequences of it not passing

26. Which of the following <u>questions is answered</u> by the passage?

    (A) Which crops are grown along the river?

    (B) Can homes be built along the river?

    (C) Will the legislation on balance be beneficial?

    (D) Are some farmers part of Green Citizens?

    (E) What is the best water level for the river?

S T O P

1. Gina: this lot is desolate. We should clear the rocks from it and plant hardy trees. Then it will no longer be desolate.

Peter: Even hardy trees cannot withstand the harsh climate here. The lot will once again become desolate if the trees are not planted properly and cared for regularly.

Peter tells Gina that:

(A) A good part of a plan will not automatically produce the desired result.
(B) The proper method here does not necessarily apply to other landscaping projects.
(C) The logical approach is not necessarily obvious.
(D) There is more than one way to accomplish a task.
(E) Some solutions are counterproductive.

2. The standard of living in Bigville has steadily increased over the past ten years even though the annual income of its residents has declined over the same period of time.

Which of the following can describe the apparent discrepancy above?

(A) Advances in technology have created conveniences people only dreamed of ten years ago.
(B) The number of residents in Bigville has declined over the past ten years.
(C) Annual income is only one factor that determines a city's standard of living.
(D) Over the past ten years the annual income in the rest of the country has declined more than it has in Bigville.
(E) Methods for calculating standard of living have changed over time.

3. All red wines from Hinterton Valley have higher acidity levels and are more popular than cheaper wines from Cantor Valley. Most Hinterton Valley white wines cost more than Cantor Valley white wines, but none of them cost as much as Cantor Valley red wines. Sparkling white wines from both valleys are cheaper than any other wine from their valley of origin.

Joseph Price, a wine that is cheaper than some Cantor Valley white wines, could be:

(A) The cheapest Cantor Valley sparkling wine.
(B) A red wine from Hinterton Valley.
(C) A Hinterton Valley white wine.
(D) The most expensive Cantor Valley red wine.
(E) A Hinterton Valley sparkling wine.

GO OVER TO THE NEXT PAGE.

4. Congress will not pass recently introduced legislation that simplifies taxes on homes because that legislation does not enjoy popular support. Most of the respondents in a nationwide survey of homeowners indicated that they oppose legislation that would change how their homes are taxed, even if their overall tax rate would remain the same.

Which of the following is an assumption upon which the above reasoning depends?

- (A) The survey accurately identified a group of voters who can establish whether the legislation has popular support.
- (B) The respondents to the nationwide survey hold views that are representative of all homeowners.
- (C) The survey is valid because people who oppose changing legislation also oppose simplifying legislation.
- (D) The survey was accurate.
- (E) The legislature will enact only legislation that has popular support.

5. It is preferable to own a young pet turtle that will live for a long time than to have a pet dog because the lifespan of a dog is substantially shorter than that of a human being. If you have a pet dog, it is likely that you will go through the grief of witnessing your pet grow old and eventually die.

The above reasoning is most closely paralleled by the argument that:

- (A) It is best to own healthy animals because they are more fun.
- (B) It is okay to live a selfish life because you only live once.
- (C) If dogs lived longer they would be better pets.
- (D) Diamond rings are preferable to cars because they last longer.
- (E) Elderly humans should own dogs instead of turtles.

6. Critic: You invest only in tanker companies that have double hulled tankers to help protect wildlife when there is an oil spill. However, those same companies also have single hulled tankers that represent a serious threat to seals, otters, and several kinds of fish. If you are serious about protecting wildlife, you should not invest in those companies.

If valid, which of these principles would most support the critic's position?

- (A) It is better to directly help a cause than to indirectly hurt such cause, even if you receive some personal benefit.
- (B) You should place your resources only in organizations that always act to further things you're serious about.
- (C) Some compromises are inevitably necessary, especially with regard to large organizations.
- (D) If a group of creatures is unable to protect itself, you should do your part to help those creatures survive.
- (E) Helping the helpless is far more rewarding than profiting from an activity that can potentially hurt the helpless.

7. Certain of the ball bearings from X Co. are flawed. It follows that, because it is of critical importance that the space station function with a minimal amount of mechanical breakdowns, no bearings from X Co. should be used on the space station.

This argument is flawed because it:

- (A) Does not distinguish between a necessary outcome and an acceptable outcome.
- (B) Confuses a spatial relationship for a causal one.
- (C) Assumes that a better result can be obtained with another approach.
- (D) Establishes a causal connection where such connection does not necessarily exist.
- (E) Draws a conclusion based on what could be isolated cases.

GO OVER TO THE NEXT PAGE.

8. The bug population in farmer Rodriguez' crops has declined consistently over the past three years despite the fact that pests in the Benitez valley, where the farm is located, have increased over the same period of time. Clearly, Mr. Rodriguez is a better farmer than his colleagues in the Benitez valley.

The above reasoning assumes:

(A) Mr. Rodriguez was responsible for the decline in the bug population of his crops.
(B) The crops grown by Mr. Rodriguez are similar to the rest of the crops grown in Benitez valley.
(C) The areas of the Benitez valley that experienced an increase in pests were farmland.
(D) Pest control, and not crop production, is a more important factor in determining whether someone is a good farmer.
(E) A decline in bug population is good, even if it is accomplished with harmful pesticides.

9. The discrepancy in bug populations can be explained by the fact that:

(A) In the past three years Mr. Rodriguez has planted different crops that are not hospitable to the bugs in the valley.
(B) Mr. Rodriguez is a good person.
(C) Mr. Rodriguez' crops yield more than those of his colleagues in the valley.
(D) The land on Mr. Rodriguez' farm is more fertile than other land in the valley.
(E) Genetically engineered crops grow despite the presence of pests.

10. Human beings possess an intuitive sense of the truth. A recent study has found that this sense of the truth extends beyond basic concepts, such as the widespread belief that murder is wrong. The study found that people were able to discern whether some facts were true when a person informed them, in a monotone voice, of various true and untrue facts.

The above argument is most strengthened by which of the following:

(A) The participants in the study were smart older people with extensive experience dealing with life issues.
(B) The results of the study were more mixed when it came to the participants' ability to discern half truths.
(C) Other studies performed on higher level primates have come to similar conclusions, albeit the truths used were simpler.
(D) A similar study arrived at a similar conclusion when participants were informed of true and untrue information through a loudspeaker.
(E) Most people are affected by a truth when they are able to discern it through their own intuition, and not when the truth is explained to them.

11. The electric utility sought to justify the 10 percent increase in utility rates by indicating that most of the increase was necessary because of the need to develop alternative forms of energy generation, such as solar energy. But, a careful analysis of the utility's expenditures shows that solar energy has, and will continue to be, a small part of the budget. Overhead costs and expenditures on coal and gas remained significant parts of the utility's budget. The utility's justification is not credible.

If true, which of the following most strengthens the conclusion that the utility's justification is not credible?

(A) This year most utilities are increasing their budget by at least 10 percent.
(B) Gas prices have increased substantially and are expected to continue to increase.
(C) It is not cost-effective to develop solar energy at this time because the technology is too undeveloped.
(D) In the past, the utility has tried to use improper justifications for rate increases.
(E) The "overhead expenses" being increased include the salary paid to the CEO.

GO OVER TO THE NEXT PAGE.

152

12. Principal: Students learn everything they know about biology from their biology professor. Thus, no student will know more than any other student if the biology professor teaches everyone effectively. If no student is more knowledgeable than other students, no student can do better than the other students. But an effective professor does not teach everything there is to know about biology. Therefore some students can know more than the rest of the students.

Which of the following explains the apparent conflict in the principal's statements?

(A) The principal is unreasonable and the conflict cannot be explained.
(B) There is no conflict because the principal is describing the initial stages in how students acquire information.
(C) The statements do not account for differences in intelligence between students and in their level of interest in biology.
(D) The principal does not consider the possibility that certain biology professors teach more biology than others and that certain environments are more biologically diverse than others.
(E) As long as an effective professor is the only source of biology information, no student will have an advantage, but that changes as students access other information sources.

13. Mr. Jones, the mayor of Pleasantville, wants to raise taxes to pay for a golden statue commemorating his achievements. Taxes should be raised to pay for more worthy causes, not to fund a useless pork-barrel project.

This argument would be weakened if:

(A) A public project's merit is determined by how popular it is, and Pleasantville supports a statute of Mr. Jones.
(B) Some of Mr. Jones' achievements have included the construction statues of famous people.
(C) Hungry homeless children are the single biggest issue facing Pleasantville.
(D) Pleasantville is a highly prosperous town that can easily afford higher taxes.
(E) A statue of Mr. Jones is a worthy cause because he is a good person.

14. From 1992 to 1996 a state program was in place under which university applicants who identified themselves as Native Americans received a substantial subsidy. During those years the number of applicants who identified themselves as Native Americans tripled, and they were enrolled in university programs at the same rate as other applicants. However, there was no increase in student participation with respect to activities commonly associated with Native Americans, such as courses on the history of Native Americans, student groups devoted to addressing Native American issues, etc. After 1996 participation in those kinds of activities remained roughly in line with what it had been during the prior decade, even though applicants identifying themselves as Native Americans declined substantially.

Which of these statements is the strongest conclusion that can be made with respect to the above information?

(A) While student participation in university programs was subsidized, Native American programs were not, and thus the new applicants found them uninteresting.
(B) It is difficult to arrive at a conclusion about participation in Native American programs because there is no clear definition of who is "Native American."
(C) The subsidy program was flawed because it simply required applicants to identify their ethnic origin, without additional proof of their origin.
(D) The subsidy program was unfair towards other disadvantaged minorities because it did not allocate any funds to those groups.
(E) The increase in Native American applicants was made up of people who were not Native American, or who are not commonly thought of as such.

GO OVER TO THE NEXT PAGE.

15. A government program to reduce pollution offers car owners the fair market value of their cars if they have emissions of pollutants that are above a certain threshold. The car owners also get a tax deduction for the amount that their vehicle is purchased for. Bob planned on taking his old and highly polluting vehicle to a junkyard and dispose of it, but instead he sold the vehicle to the government under the program. With the money he bought a large SUV that pollutes more than a vehicle he would have purchased without the money from the government.

If the above is true, the government program must:

(A) have been enacted for the wrong reasons because it does not benefit the government or the environment.

(B) be changed so that people who are thinking about junking their vehicles do not get money from the government.

(C) create more pollution in certain circumstances than would exist had the program not been enacted.

(D) be repealed because, rather than lowering pollution, it actually increases the level of pollution emitted by cars.

(E) impose a penalty on Bob because he is unfairly taking advantage of a situation that he has contributed to.

16. John: Obeying the speed limit is of no value. Even if we had obeyed the speed limit we would still have been involved in the accident by the big bend last year. The speed limit does not address the root problems of highway safety.

Margret: Any rule that could possibly help drivers is useful. The speed limit prevents certain crashes. Whenever a crash occurs there is a potential for people to be injured and property to be damaged.

Margret indicates:

(A) The speed limit's utility should be evaluated in light of additional considerations.

(B) There are other reasons why last year's accident could have been avoided.

(C) The proper speed limit in one case may be used in other cases.

(D) John incorrectly assumes that driving a different speed would have avoided last year's accident.

(E) John fails to take into account an important distinction between actual usefulness and possible usefulness.

17. Tall people, who society routinely rewards with influential positions, do not appreciate the difficulties shorter people face. Studies have found that most women want to date men who are taller than themselves. It is not a coincidence that Abraham Lincoln was a tall person because voters tend to elect tall officials. Society does a disservice to itself by giving weight to an arbitrary feature that people have no control over and that bears no connection to the task of performing the duties of influential positions.

The above conclusion depends on the following assumption:

(A) People's interests are served when a person's ability to perform a duty is given weight, regardless of people's preferences.

(B) Society should give other characteristics, such as a person's accomplishments, more weight.

(C) Short people are as capable as tall people.

(D) Most tall people are appointed to positions for which they are not qualified.

(E) There probably was a shorter person who could have been a better president than Abraham Lincoln.

GO OVER TO THE NEXT PAGE.

154

18. Teacher: the deepest truths are often the most obvious ones, which people do not acknowledge because they are also inconvenient truths.

Which of the following principles most closely conforms to the principle expressed above?

(A) Solutions to exam questions may be placed in an exam itself because people will not read them anyway, even if they do not know the answer to an exam question.

(B) Some of the best solutions to poverty, such as honest government, are not implemented because they are not in everyone's interests.

(C) If you take time to stop and think of the many good things you have, you will be more grateful and have a better understanding of what you should do with your life.

(D) The best inventions that have been made occurred because an inventor took a seemingly ordinary object and turned it into something extraordinary.

(E) Pain can be a professor if, through discernment, you carefully examine difficult situations of the past and gain strength from them for the future.

19. Politician: The use of military force is appropriate when only the aggressor feels the effects of such force. Military force is not appropriate when it affects innocent people and when it is expensive.

Which of the following is most supported by the position articulated by the politician?

(A) The invasion of country A impacted most, but not all, the aggressors. Therefore, if it was not expensive, it was appropriate.

(B) The invasion of country Q impacted only a few aggressors and was expensive. It was therefore inappropriate.

(C) The use of military force in country S is highly expensive. If it does not affect aggressors, it is inappropriate.

(D) The use of military force in country B was inexpensive, but did not affect many aggressors. Therefore it was not appropriate.

(E) Sending troops to the capital of country X affected only aggressors and no innocent people. It was thus appropriate.

20. John: I oppose the death penalty because killing people is immoral, no matter what the circumstances.

Peter: I support the death penalty because sometimes it is necessary to execute people to save other lives.

John's argument would be strengthened if:

(A) It is not humanly possible to determine when lives can be saved by killing people.

(B) Most people believe that killing people is immoral.

(C) The death penalty has never, in fact, saved lives.

(D) Even with advances in DNA science, people are still mistakenly given the death penalty.

(E) Giving people a life sentence is sufficient punishment for even the worst of crimes.

GO OVER TO THE NEXT PAGE.

155

21. Most people from infancy have one main language that they speak. When they learn another language they invariably speak that language with the accent of their first language. In today's globalized economy, many people are beginning to speak two languages throughout their formative years. When they learn a third language they usually speak it with less of an accent, even if the language is not related to the family of languages of their first two languages.

From the information above one can most strongly conclude that:

    (A) People who know only one language in their formative years are not as motivated as others to learn another language.

    (B) People who know two languages are smarter than people who know only one language.

    (C) Knowing three languages in your formative years makes language acquisition even more easy.

    (D) Knowing two languages well can help people to communicate in a third language.

    (E) If you know only one language, the best way to learn a hard language is to first learn an easier one.

22. Teacher: The head coach of the most successful football team in the state told me that his best players studied football strategies in class. Therefore, to make our team better I suggest that we have them attend football classes.

All of the following would, if true, weaken the teacher's reasoning about the football classes EXCEPT:

    (A) Football strategies are best taught on the football field during practice.

    (B) Morale of a game is important for winning and sitting in a class hurts a football team's morale.

    (C) While some players improve in class, most football positions simply require brute force.

    (D) Most football teachers have a limited understanding of how strategies are implemented.

    (E) Taking football classes is an interesting and stimulating activity for most teams.

23. Traffic on the winding two lane Taterbed road through the Pierlight mountain pass is always congested because large slow trucks do not allow faster cars to safely pass. The road would be much safer if it were widened to four lanes.

Which of the following is an assumption upon which the above reasoning depends?

    (A) It is possible for cars to drive through the Pierlight pass at both higher speeds and in a safer manner.

    (B) The Taterbed road will be safer if it is less congested.

    (C) It is possible to widen the Taterbed road to four lanes.

    (D) More cars and trucks will not travel on the Taterbed road if it is widened to four lanes.

    (E) Roads with more lanes are safer.

24. Critic: None of the several witnesses to the recent gas truck collision are credible because they each have a different opinion as to the cause of the accident. The witnesses are either trying to further their own agenda, or they were not paying attention when the accident occurred. Thus, they are not reliable.

The critic's argument is flawed because:

    (A) There are other reasons that could explain why the witnesses have different opinions about such an accident.

    (B) It concludes, based on a difference as to one aspect of the crash, that the witnesses are entirely not credible.

    (C) It is insensitive to the fact that the accident may have been traumatic and thus affected the perceptions of the witnesses.

    (D) If the witnesses' opinions are not taken into account, we will not have a full picture of what occurred in the accident.

    (E) The uncertainties caused by the inconsistent accounts could be reconciled by using physical evidence from the crash.

GO OVER TO THE NEXT PAGE.

21. Most people from infancy have one main language that they speak. When they learn another language they invariably speak that language with the accent of their first language. In today's globalized economy, many people are beginning to speak two languages throughout their formative years. When they learn a third language they usually speak it with less of an accent, even if the language is not related to the family of languages of their first two languages.

From the information above one can most strongly conclude that:

(A) People who know only one language in their formative years are not as motivated as others to learn another language.

(B) People who know two languages are smarter than people who know only one language.

(C) Knowing three languages in your formative years makes language acquisition even more easy.

(D) Knowing two languages well can help people to communicate in a third language.

(E) If you know only one language, the best way to learn a hard language is to first learn an easier one.

22. Teacher: The head coach of the most successful football team in the state told me that his best players studied football strategies in class. Therefore, to make our team better I suggest that we have them attend football classes.

All of the following would, if true, weaken the teacher's reasoning about the football classes EXCEPT:

(A) Football strategies are best taught on the football field during practice.

(B) Morale of a game is important for winning and sitting in a class hurts a football team's morale.

(C) While some players improve in class, most football positions simply require brute force.

(D) Most football teachers have a limited understanding of how strategies are implemented.

(E) Taking football classes is an interesting and stimulating activity for most teams.

23. Traffic on the winding two lane Taterbed road through the Pierlight mountain pass is always congested because large slow trucks do not allow faster cars to safely pass. The road would be much safer if it were widened to four lanes.

Which of the following is an assumption upon which the above reasoning depends?

(A) It is possible for cars to drive through the Pierlight pass at both higher speeds and in a safer manner.

(B) The Taterbed road will be safer if it is less congested.

(C) It is possible to widen the Taterbed road to four lanes.

(D) More cars and trucks will not travel on the Taterbed road if it is widened to four lanes.

(E) Roads with more lanes are safer.

24. Critic: None of the several witnesses to the recent gas truck collision are credible because they each have a different opinion as to the cause of the accident. The witnesses are either trying to further their own agenda, or they were not paying attention when the accident occurred. Thus, they are not reliable.

The critic's argument is flawed because:

(A) There are other reasons that could explain why the witnesses have different opinions about such an accident.

(B) It concludes, based on a difference as to one aspect of the crash, that the witnesses are entirely not credible.

(C) It is insensitive to the fact that the accident may have been traumatic and thus affected the perceptions of the witnesses.

(D) If the witnesses' opinions are not taken into account, we will not have a full picture of what occurred in the accident.

(E) The uncertainties caused by the inconsistent accounts could be reconciled by using physical evidence from the crash.

GO OVER TO THE NEXT PAGE.

157

25. Journalists believe multinationals are taking advantage of the labor force in Province X. This is an erroneous view because most people believe journalists' views about multinationals are mistaken.

The conclusion can be critiqued because:

(A) The phrase "taking advantage" is unclear.
(B) Journalists as a group do not have cohesive views.
(C) The author arrives at the conclusion based only upon the view of "most people."
(D) The conclusion is based on the assumption that journalists cannot properly evaluate a situation.
(E) It assumes that what is true of one multinational is true of all of them.

26. Mr. Lozano, a high profile artist from Bolivia, has four basic kinds of subject matter that he paints: landscapes, seascapes, birds and cars. He also places either men or women in his paintings, but not both. A museum curator has also observed that Mr. Lozano always places women in his paintings of birds.

Which of the following must be true about Mr. Lozano's art if the above statements are true?

(A) If Mr. Lozano does a painting of birds, he does not place men in the painting.
(B) Mr. Lozano's paintings of cars do not have women in them.
(C) None of the artist's paintings combine seascapes and birds.
(D) If men are in a painting, then its subject matter is either cars or landscapes.
(E) The artist would benefit by significantly expanding the range of his subject matter.

STOP

158

①

35 minutes

Mary uses only six spices when she cooks: cumin, salt, basil, paprika, oregano and cinnamon. Her culinary rules only allow her to use the spices as follows:
Basil and paprika cannot be used together.
Basil and cumin cannot be used together.
When Mary uses oregano, she cannot also use paprika, cumin or basil.

1. Which of these could Mary use together:

(A) paprika and cumin
(B) oregano and cumin
(C) basil and cumin
(D) basil and paprika
(E) oregano and paprika

2. If Mary is not using salt or cinnamon, but is using two spices, which of the following is all of the spices Mary CANNOT use?

(A) oregano
(B) basil
(C) oregano and basil
(D) paprika and cumin
(E) basil and paprika

3. Mary CANNOT use:

(A) salt and oregano
(B) paprika and cumin
(C) oregano while using three other spices
(D) basil while using two other spices
(E) cumin while using three other spices

4. Mary must use:

(A) at most, three other spices when using oregano
(B) at most, five spices
(C) salt with at least one other spice
(D) at most, three spices
(E) at most, four spices

5. If Mary uses two spices, what are the total number of combinations she could be using?

(A) 9
(B) 10
(C) 12
(D) 7
(E) 14

6. If Mary is not allowed to use less than a total of three spices under her rules, which of the following must be true:

(A) Mary is using salt and cumin.
(B) Mary is not using oregano.
(C) Mary is using cinnamon, but not basil.
(D) Mary is using paprika or cumin.
(E) Mary is using salt, or cinnamon, or both salt and cinnamon.

spices
cu, s, b, p, o, ci

GO OVER TO THE NEXT PAGE.

(cu, b, p → ∅)

② cu, s, b, p, o, ci

④ s, ci, p, cu

⑤ s/ci, sb, sp, so, s/cu
ci/b, ci/p, ci/o, ci/cu
p/cu

159

A teacher tutors nine children: B, F, H, I, N, P, R, S, and V. The children are tutored one at a time, once a day. Each child is tutored in one sitting. The teacher teaches the children according to the following rules:

S and V are both taught before H.
N and B are both taught before P.
R is taught after P, but before F.
I is taught at some point before F.

7. It is possible that:

   (A) F is the fifth person taught.
   (B) N is the seventh person taught.
   (C) B is the eighth person taught.
   (D) I is the eighth person taught.
   (E) P is the ninth person taught.

8. If H is taught fourth, any of the following could be taught third, EXCEPT:

   (A) I
   (B) R
   (C) B
   (D) N
   (E) V

9. Which child CANNOT be taught fourth?

   (A) R
   (B) H
   (C) P
   (D) B
   (E) F

10. If F is taught sixth, then which of the following must be correct?

    (A) S is taught seventh.
    (B) I is taught fifth.
    (C) H is taught ninth.
    (D) N is taught first.
    (E) P is taught third.

11. If S is the sixth person that is taught, which of these must be correct?

    (A) H is taught after P.
    (B) V is taught before F.
    (C) I is taught after R.
    (D) R is taught before V.
    (E) N is taught after B.

12. If V is taught fifth, which one of these could be correct?

    (A) N is taught after R.
    (B) V is taught before B.
    (C) H is taught before N.
    (D) P is taught after H.
    (E) F is taught right after V.

GO OVER TO THE NEXT PAGE.

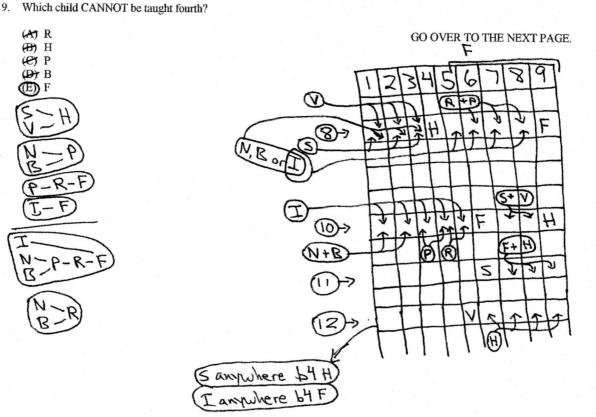

160

Four general practitioners – Drs. Barnerdale, Eavedorn; Artnarp, and Coopersman -- and three specialists -- Drs. Marstervel, Ostwawill, and Partnit each see patients once a day in one of two clinics – Arsbald and Bodt. Each doctor sees patients for exactly one half hour. The clinics are right next to each other and are open for patient visits only during these times: Arsbald at 1 p.m., 1:30 p.m. and 2 p.m., and Bodt at 1:30 p.m., 2 p.m., 2:30 p.m. and 3 p.m.

The doctors see their patients according to these rules:

Dr. Barnerdale sees patients right before a specialist, but not necessarily in the same clinic.

Drs. Coopersman and Ostwawill see patients in different clinics.

If a specialist sees someone at 1:30 p.m., no general practitioner sees anyone at that time.

Dr. Artnarp sees patients at some point in time before Dr. Eavedorn.

Dr. Coopersman sees patients at either 1 p.m. or 3 p.m.

13. If a specialist sees a patient at 1:30 p.m. then which of these must be true?

(A) Coopersman cannot be in a time slot right before Ostwawill.
(B) Barnerdale must see patients at 2 p.m.
(C) Artnarp cannot be scheduled at 1 p.m.
(D) Barnerdale cannot schedule patients at 2:30 p.m.
(E) Marstervel and Partnit must be scheduled at 1:30 p.m.

14. If Barnerdale sees patients at 1 p.m. which could be a proper scheduling of doctors at Bodt from 1:30 p.m. to 2:30 p.m.?

(A) Marstervel, Partnit, Eavedorn
(B) Marstervel, Eavedorn, Partnit
(C) Ostwawill, Artnarp, Eavedorn
(D) Artnarp, Eavedorn, Partnit
(E) Eavedorn, Marstervel, Partnit

15. Which doctors must see patients before 2:30 p.m.?

(A) Coopersman and Artnarp
(B) Ostwawill and Barnerdale
(C) Coopersman and Partnit
(D) Marstervel and Ostwawill
(E) Barnerdale and Artnarp

16. Which of these could be the schedule for Arsbald?

(A) Artnarp, Eavedorn, Partnit
(B) Coopersman, Partnit, Barnerdale
(C) Marstervel, Partnit and Ostwawill
(D) Ostwawill, Marstervel and Artnarp
(E) Barnerdale, Ostwawill and Eavedorn

17. Which doctors may see patients at 2:30 p.m. if Partnit is scheduled at 3 p.m. and if Eavedorn must see patients right after Artnarp?

(A) Barnerdale
(B) Artnarp
(C) Eavedorn
(D) Coopersman
(E) Ostwawill

18. If Barnerdale sees patients at 2 p.m., which of the following must be true?

(A) Eavedorn sees patients at 2 p.m.
(B) A specialist cannot see patients at 3 p.m.
(C) Coopersman sees patients at 3 p.m.
(D) Barnerdale sees patients in Bodt.
(E) Ostwawill sees patients at 2:30 p.m.

GO OVER TO THE NEXT PAGE.

161

Seven teachers teach in a vocational school: Ronald, Steve, Valerie, Wayne, Zeba, Alice and Marcia. Each teacher teaches one or more of these four classes: woodworking, auto repair, bricklaying and electronics.

They teach according to these conditions:
Valerie and only four other teachers teach bricklaying.
Steve teaches electronics and woodworking.
Alice doesn't teach any course that Steve teaches.
Marcia teaches more kinds of classes than Steve.
Zeba doesn't teach any course that Alice teaches.
Ronald teaches exactly three courses.

19. Which teachers can teach exactly the same courses as each other?

    (A) Marcia and Alice
    (B) Marcia and Steve
    (C) Alice and Wayne
    (D) Steve and Alice
    (E) Alice and Ronald

20. Which of these must be correct?

    (A) Ronald and Marcia teach the same courses, but neither of them teach bricklaying.
    (B) Steve and Alice teach the same courses, but neither teaches auto repair.
    (C) Valerie and Wayne teach bricklaying and auto repair, but not electronics or woodworking.
    (D) Alice teaches either auto repair, or bricklaying, or both auto repair and bricklaying.
    (E) Ronald and Steve teach the same number of courses, but do not teach bricklaying

21. Which of these cannot be correct?

    (A) Valerie teaches two courses.
    (B) Ronald and Steve teach woodworking.
    (C) Alice and Steve teach the same number of courses.
    (D) Marcia teaches as many courses as Ronald.
    (E) Marcia teaches as many courses as Alice

22. Wayne must teach:

    (A) at least two classes
    (B) bricklaying
    (C) all courses that Valerie teaches
    (D) electronics
    (E) at least two classes that Marcia teaches

23. Which of the following is a complete list of all teachers who can teach all courses?

    (A) Valerie, Wayne, Marcia
    (B) Marcia and Wayne
    (C) Valerie, Wayne, Marcia, Steve
    (D) Zeba, Valerie, Wayne, Marcia
    (E) Alice, Ronald, Valerie

[Handwritten annotations:]

teachers / courses
R, S, V, W, Z, A, M / w, ar, b, e

A teach course → S teach course
M # of classes > 2, which is 3 or 4
A teach course → Z teach course

Ae Aw Ab

S T O P

b = V, Z, R, W, M

V + 4 teachers = b
Se + w
S teach class → A teach class
M # of classes > S # of classes
Z teach class → A teach class
R = 3 classes